D0911332

221 Sycamore St.

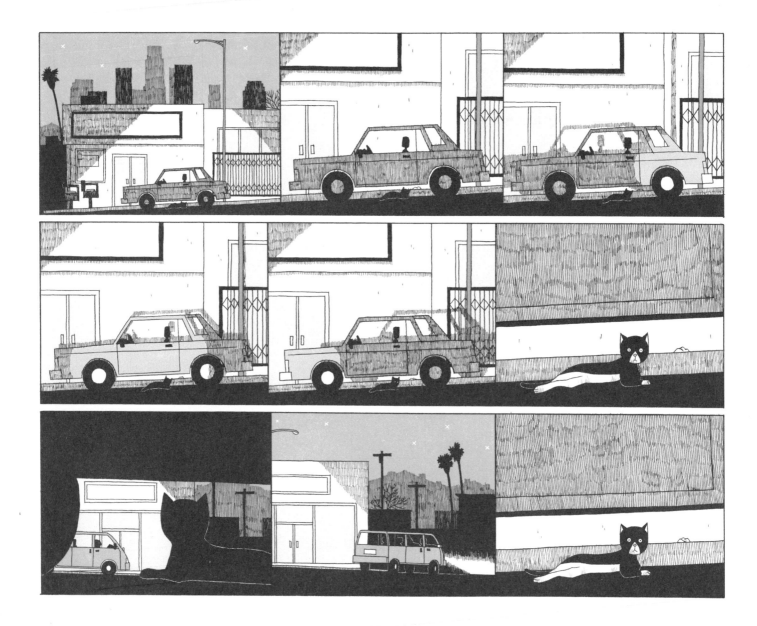

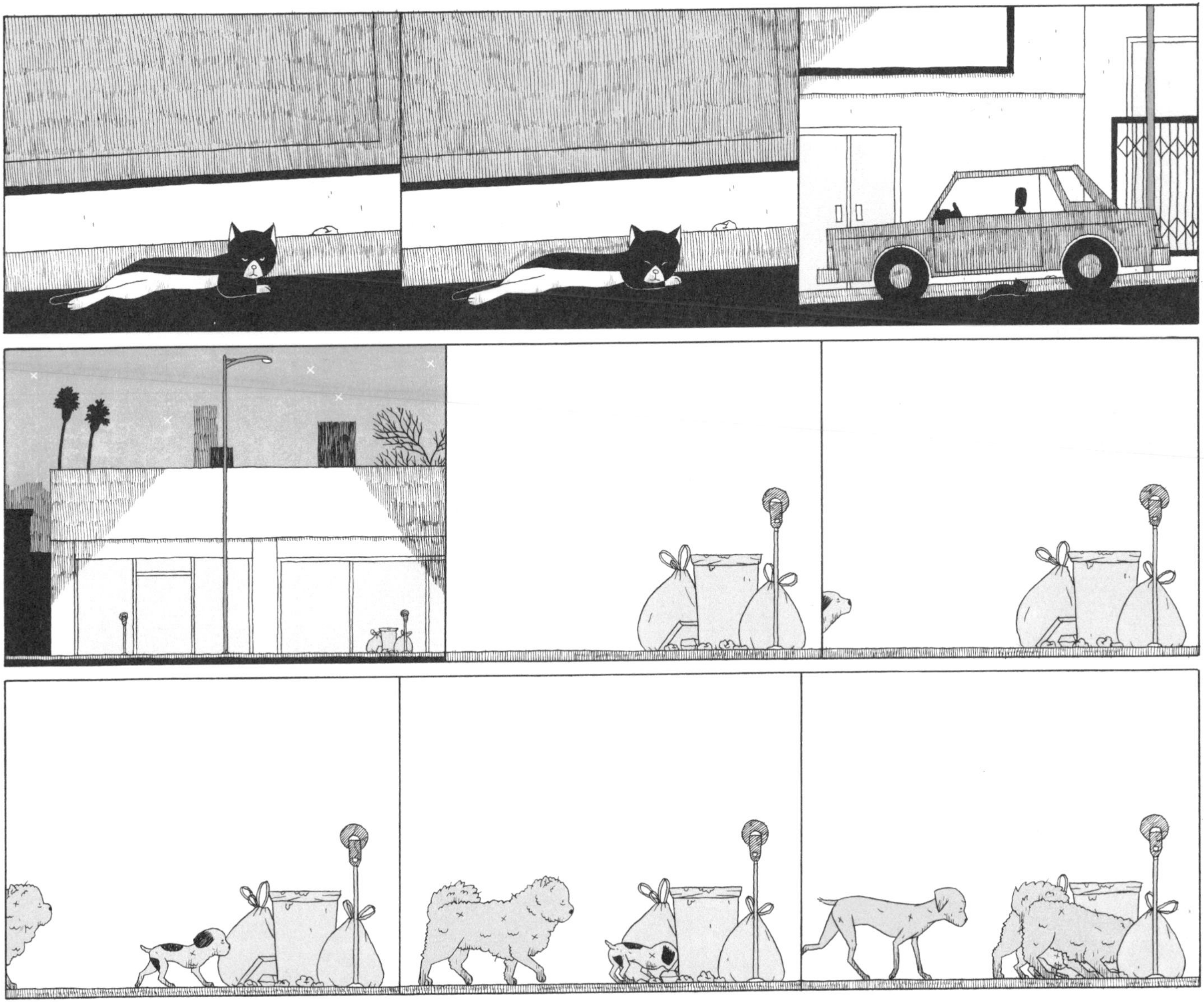

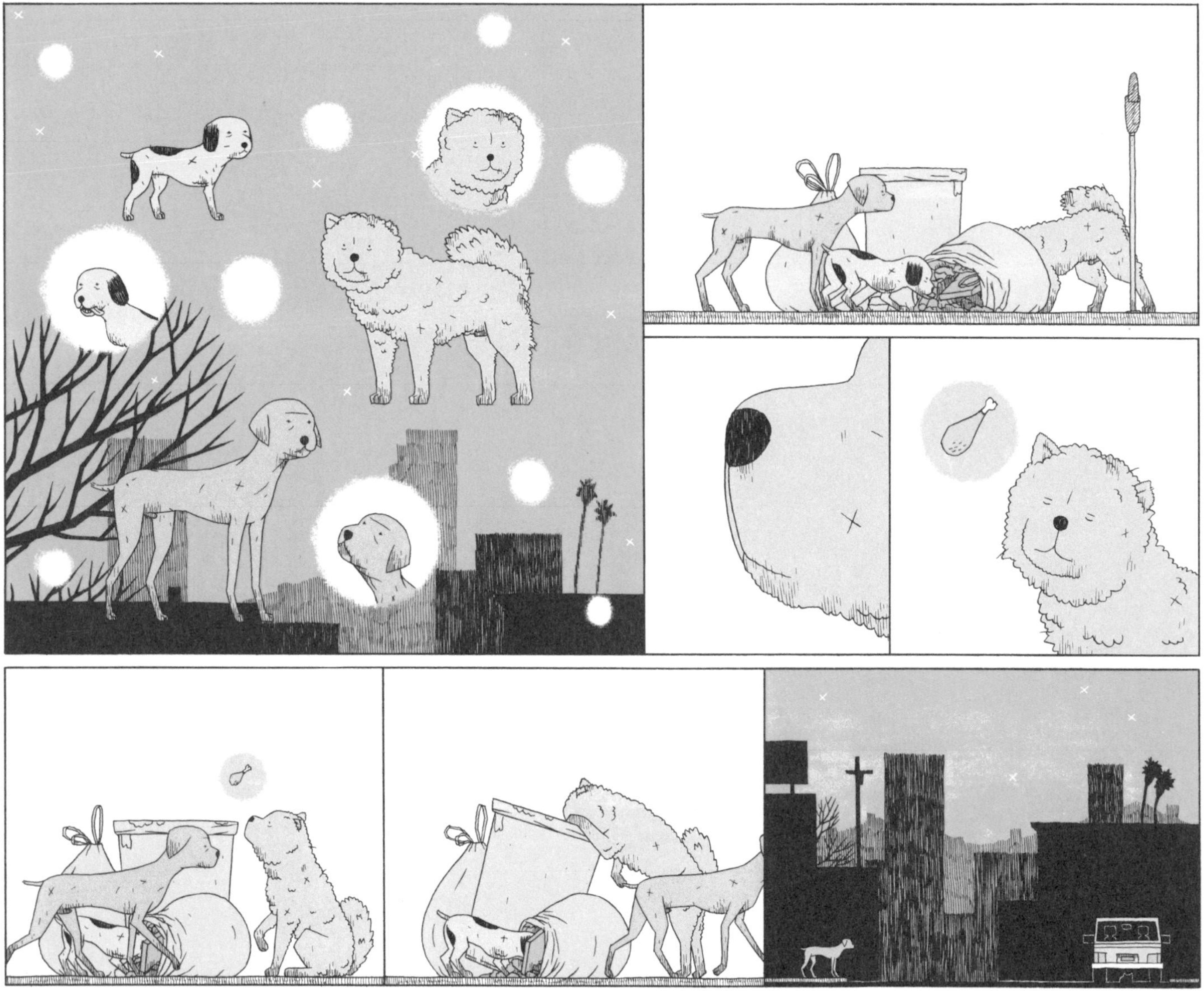

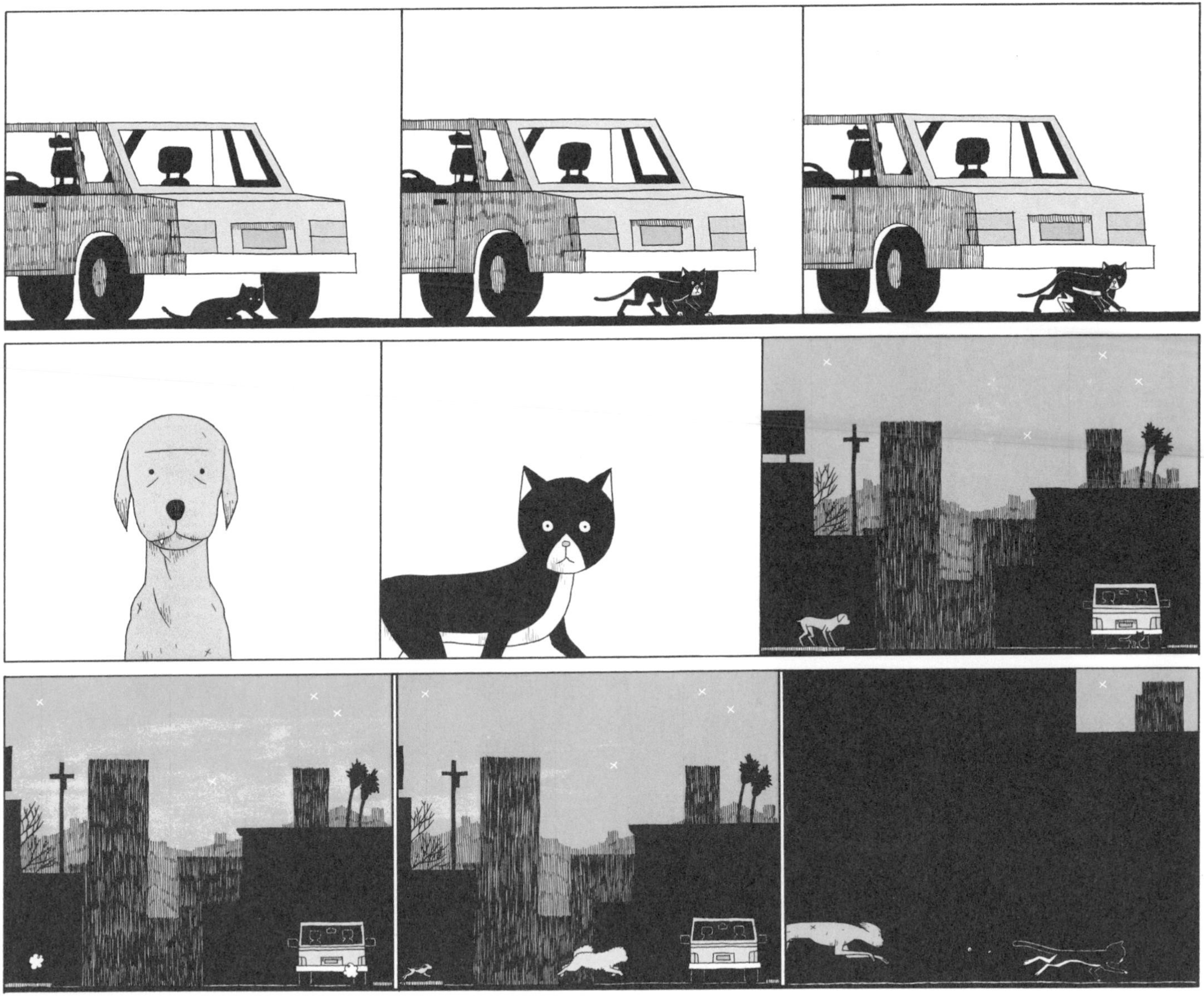

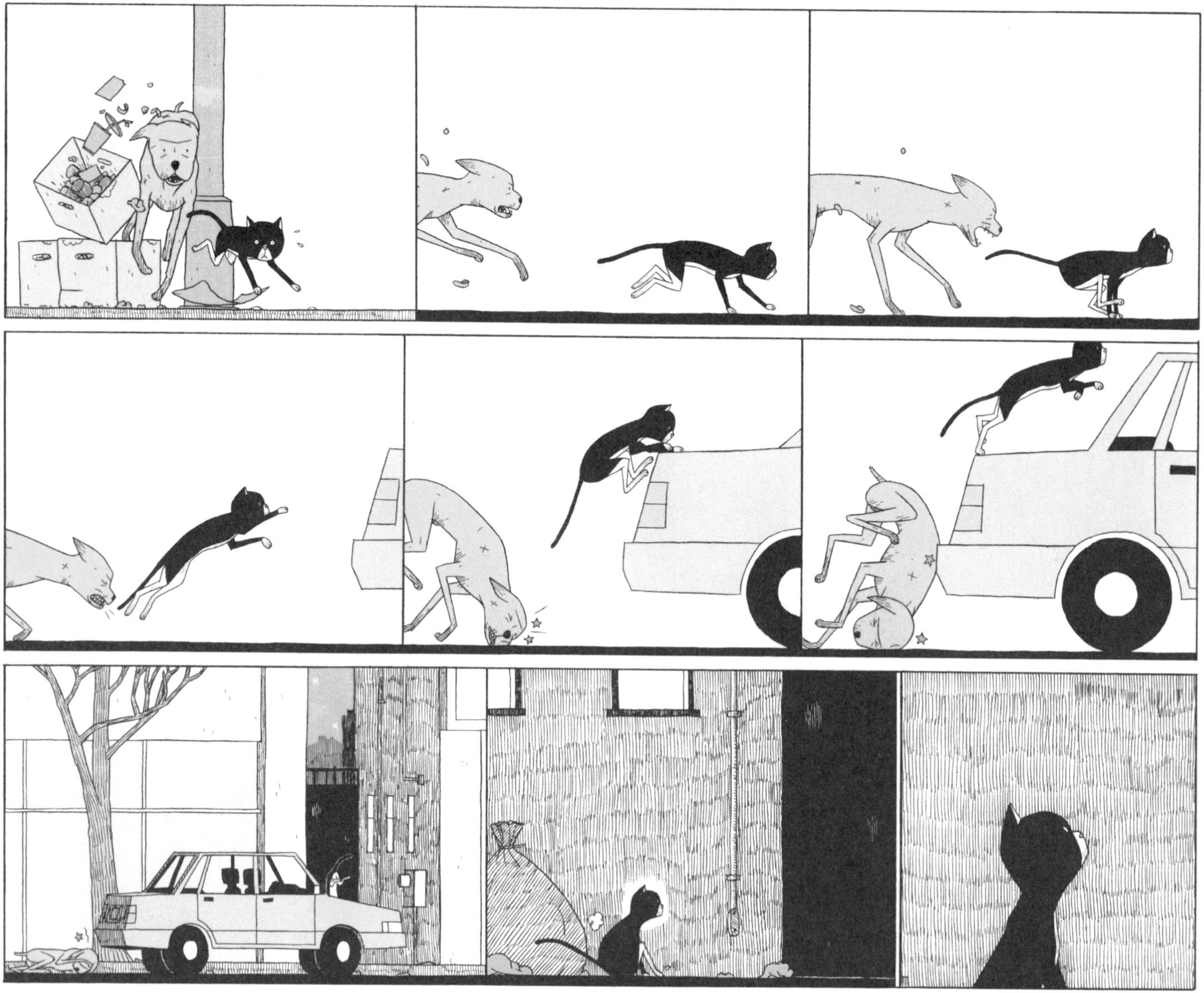

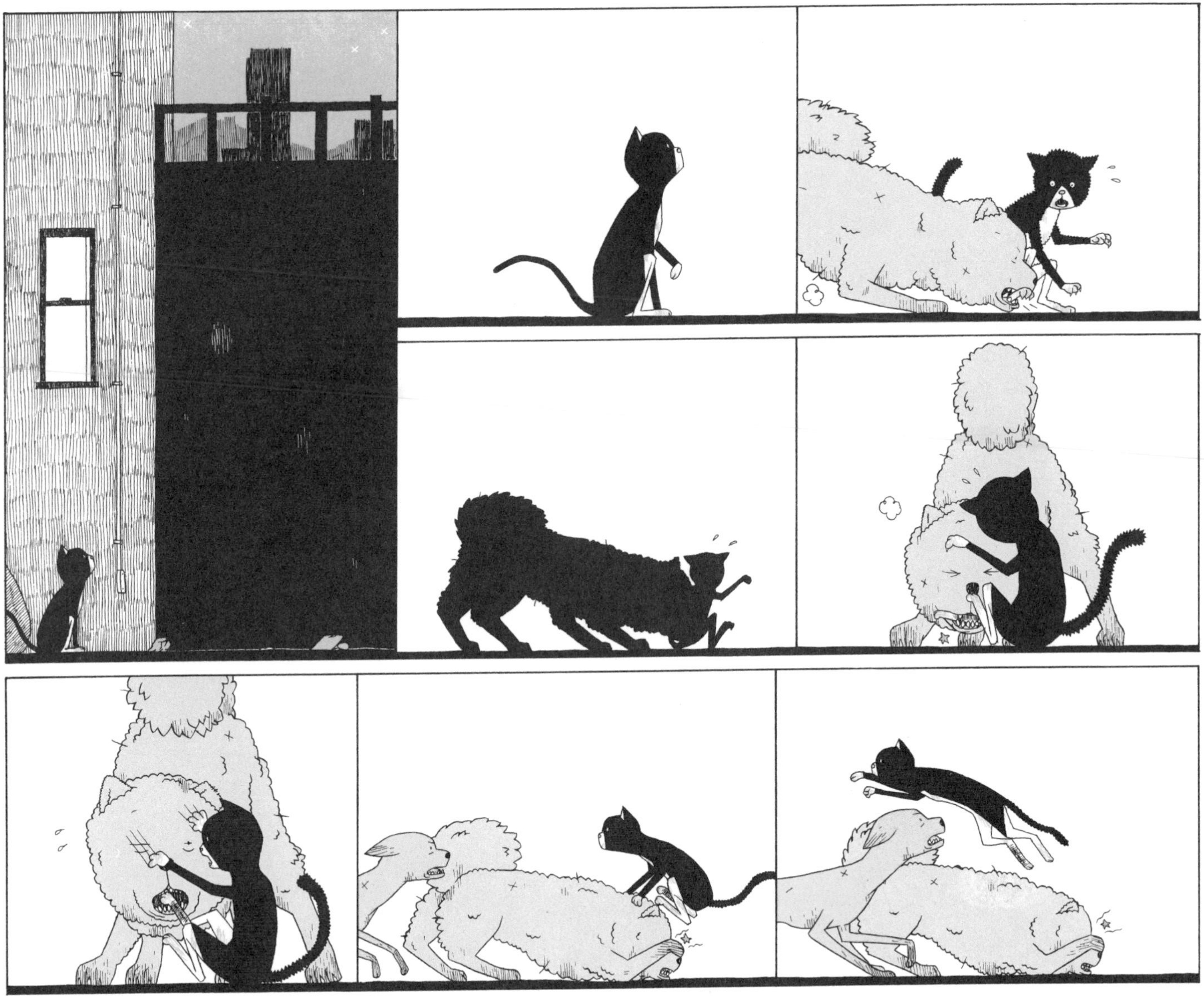

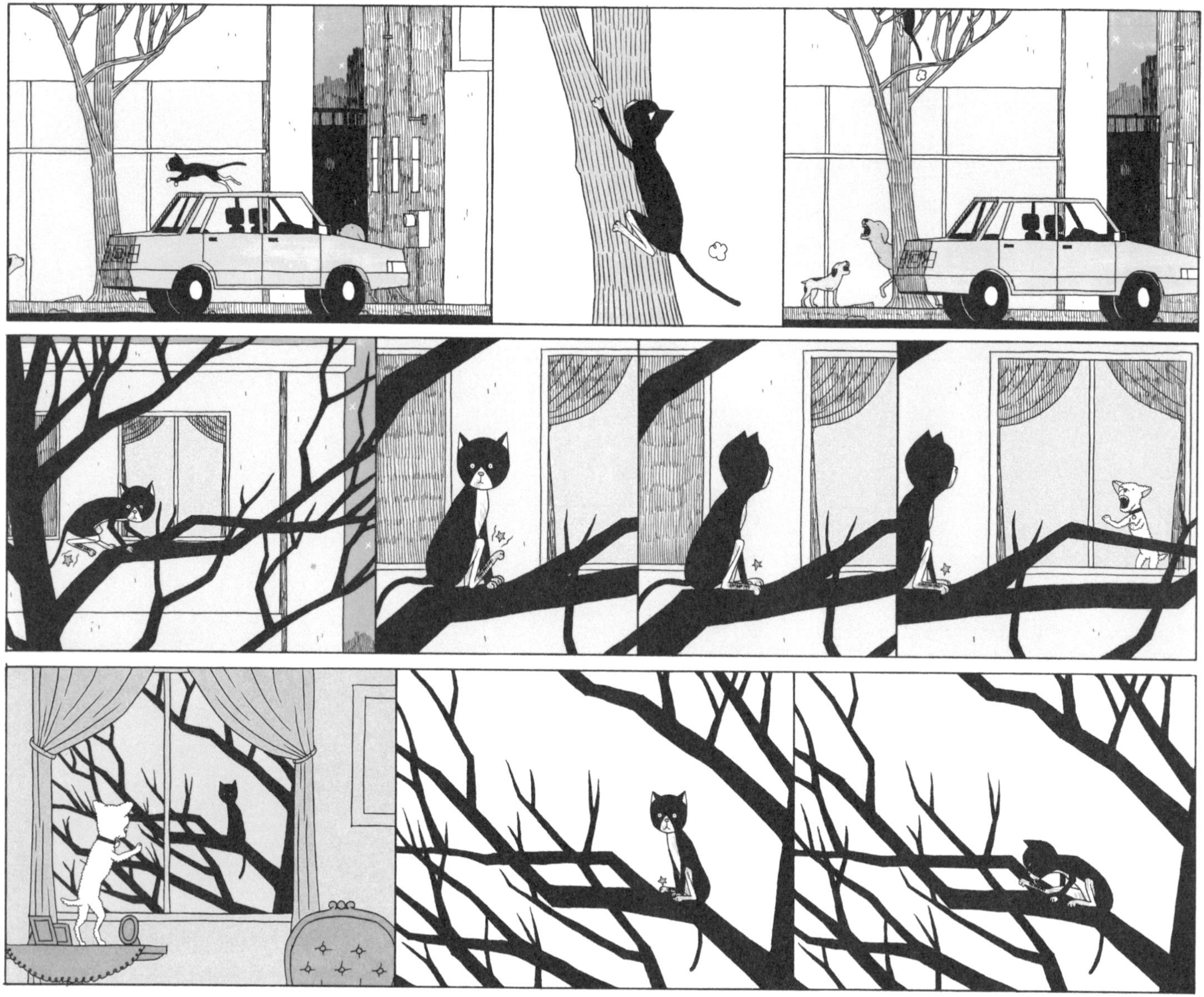

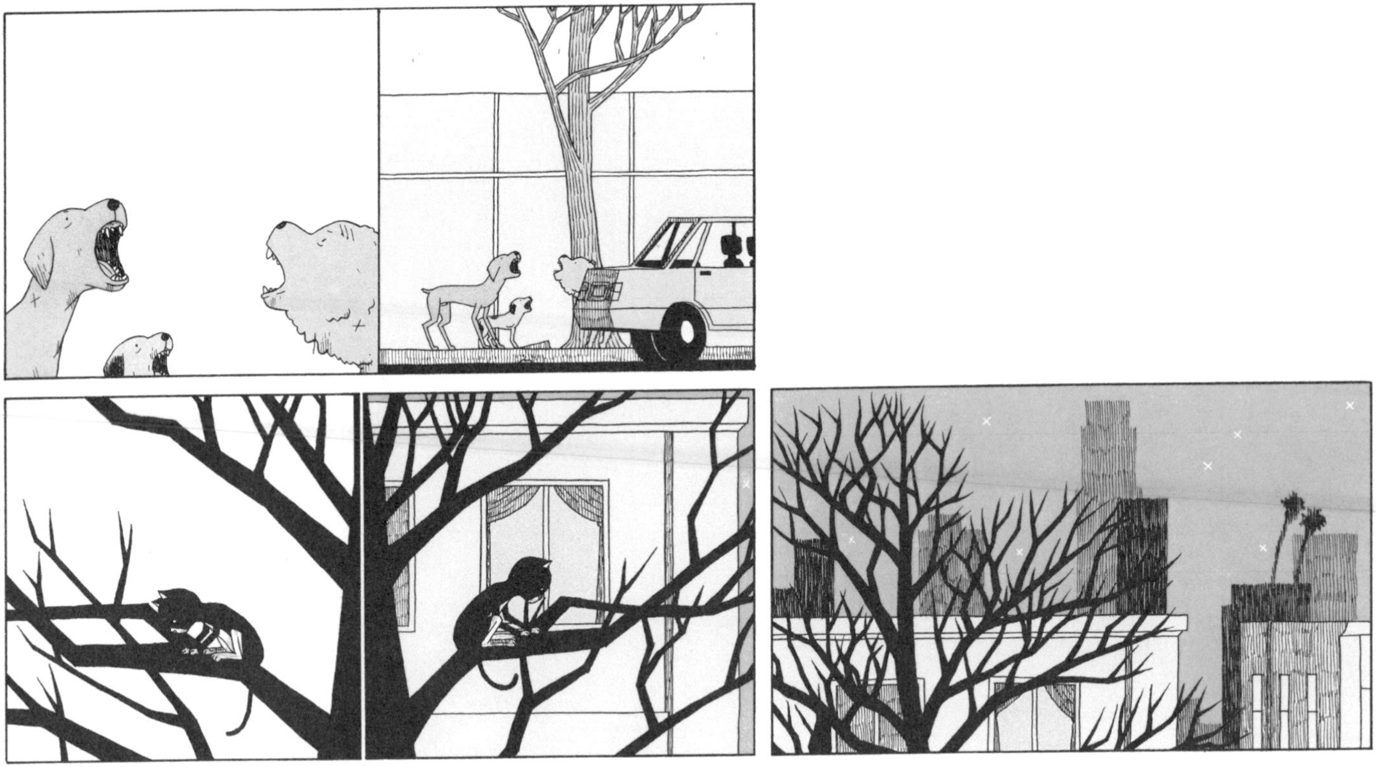

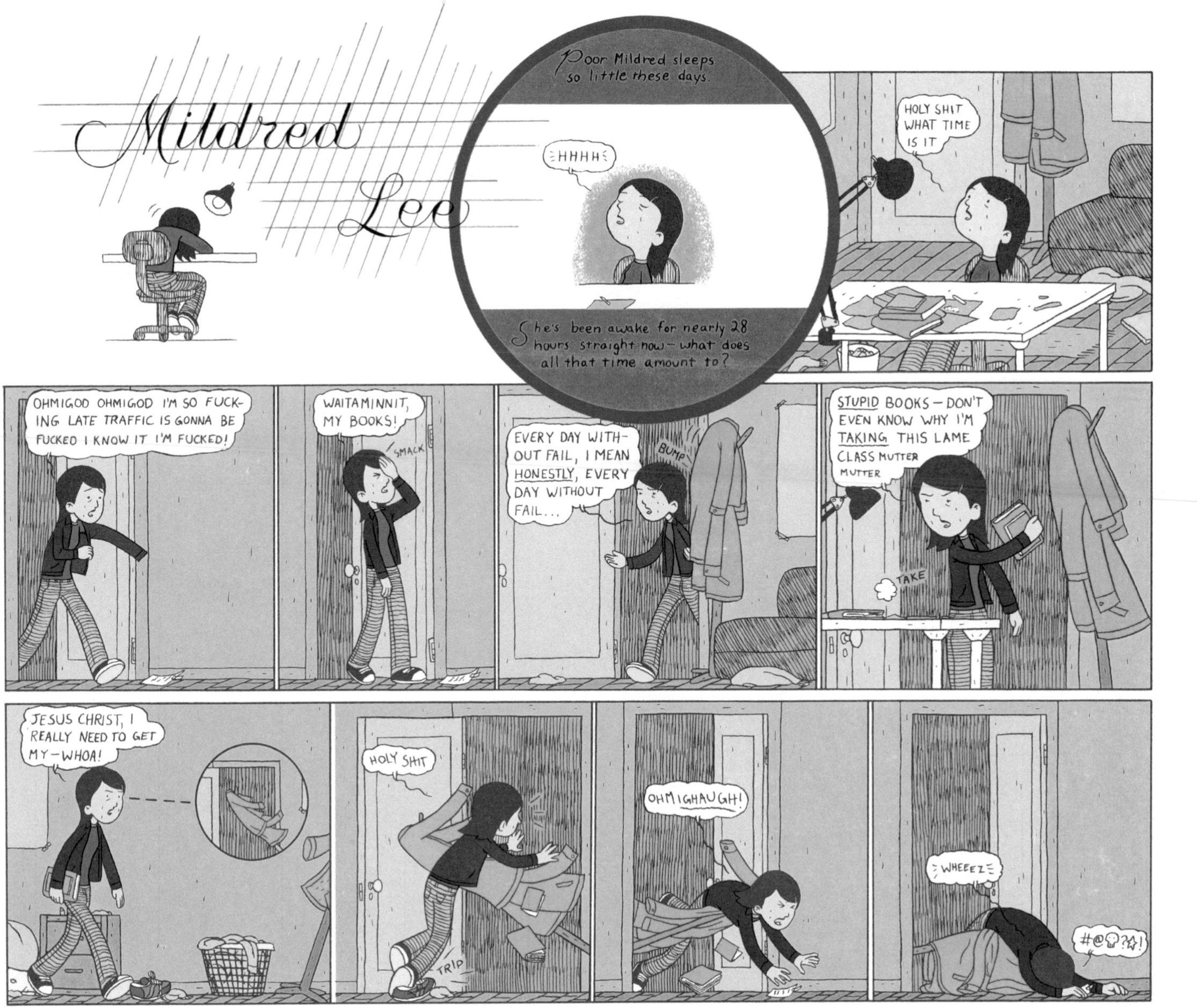
Mildred Lee
Poor Mildred sleeps so little these days.
HHHH
She's been awake for nearly 28 hours straight now—what does all that time amount to?
HOLY SHIT WHAT TIME IS IT
OHMIGOD OHMIGOD I'M SO FUCKING LATE TRAFFIC IS GONNA BE FUCKED I KNOW IT I'M FUCKED!
WAITAMINNIT, MY BOOKS!
SMACK
EVERY DAY WITHOUT FAIL, I MEAN HONESTLY, EVERY DAY WITHOUT FAIL...
BUMP
STUPID BOOKS—DON'T EVEN KNOW WHY I'M TAKING THIS LAME CLASS MUTTER MUTTER
TAKE
JESUS CHRIST, I REALLY NEED TO GET MY—WHOA!
HOLY SHIT
TRIP
OHMIGHAUGH!
WHEEEZ
#@?!

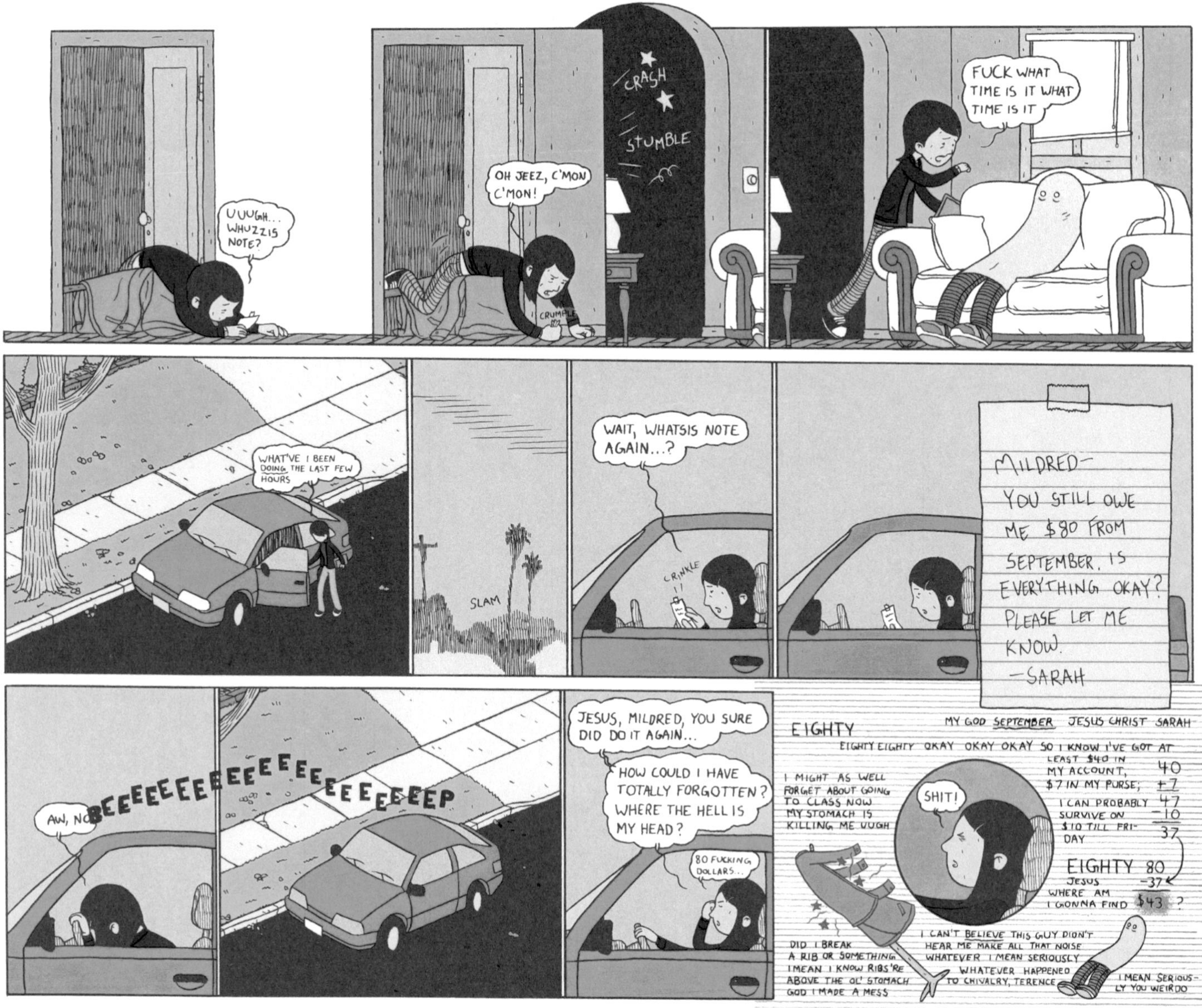
UUUGH... WHUZZIS NOTE?
OH JEEZ, C'MON C'MON!
CRUMPLE
CRASH
STUMBLE
FUCK WHAT TIME IS IT WHAT TIME IS IT
WHAT'VE I BEEN DOING THE LAST FEW HOURS
SLAM
WAIT, WHATSIS NOTE AGAIN...?
CRINKLE
MILDRED—
YOU STILL OWE ME $80 FROM SEPTEMBER. IS EVERYTHING OKAY? PLEASE LET ME KNOW.
—SARAH
AW, NO
BEEEEEEEEEEEEEEEEEEEEEEP
JESUS, MILDRED, YOU SURE DID DO IT AGAIN...
HOW COULD I HAVE TOTALLY FORGOTTEN? WHERE THE HELL IS MY HEAD?
80 FUCKING DOLLARS...
EIGHTY
MY GOD SEPTEMBER JESUS CHRIST SARAH
EIGHTY EIGHTY OKAY OKAY OKAY SO I KNOW I'VE GOT AT LEAST $40 IN MY ACCOUNT, 40
$7 IN MY PURSE; +7
47
I CAN PROBABLY SURVIVE ON $10 TILL FRIDAY -10
37
EIGHTY 80
JESUS -37
WHERE AM I GONNA FIND $43?
I MIGHT AS WELL FORGET ABOUT GOING TO CLASS NOW MY STOMACH IS KILLING ME UUGH
SHIT!
DID I BREAK A RIB OR SOMETHING I MEAN I KNOW RIBS'RE ABOVE THE OL' STOMACH GOD I MADE A MESS
I CAN'T BELIEVE THIS GUY DIDN'T HEAR ME MAKE ALL THAT NOISE WHATEVER I MEAN SERIOUSLY WHATEVER HAPPENED TO CHIVALRY, TERENCE
I MEAN SERIOUSLY YOU WEIRDO

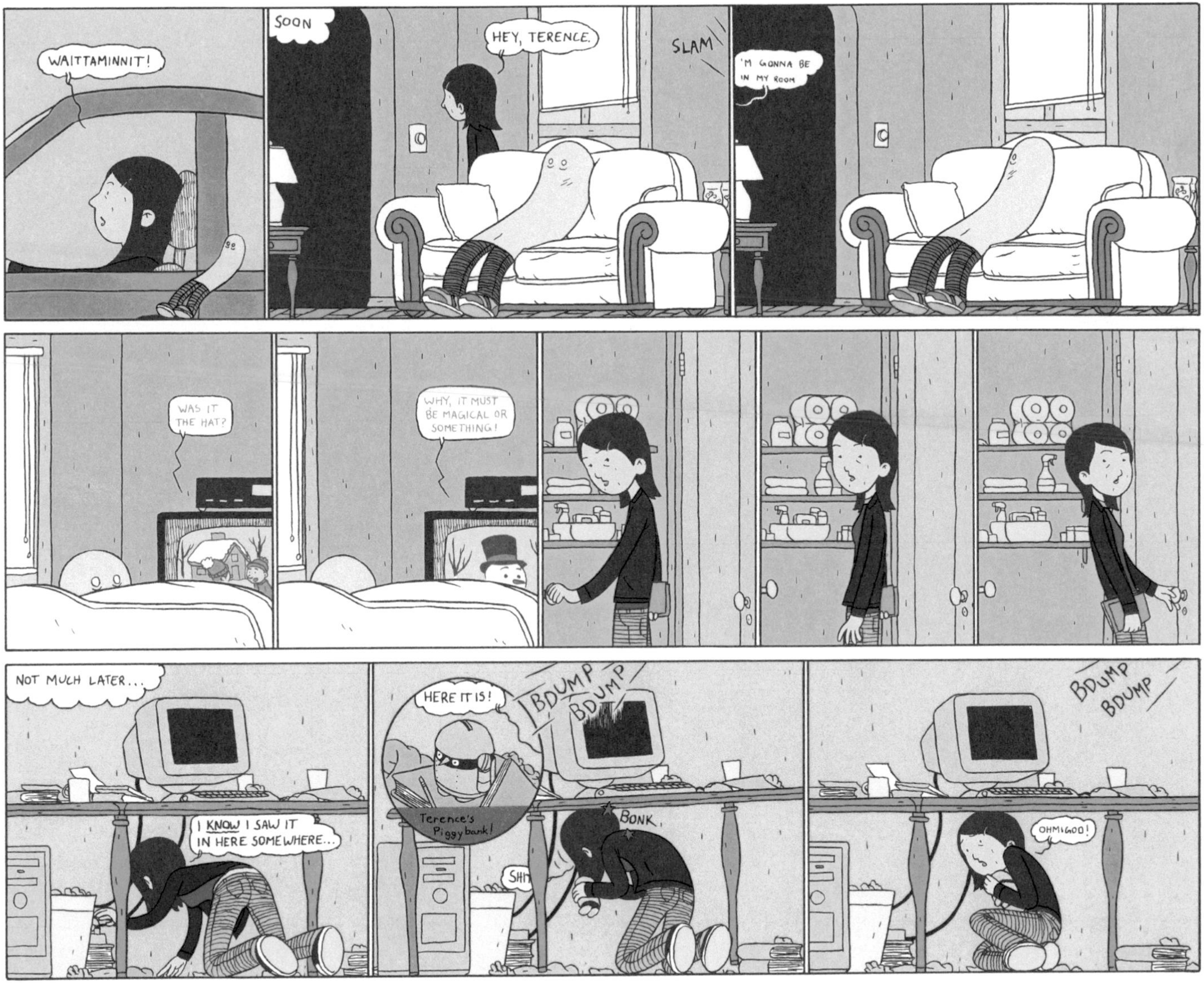

WAITTAMINNIT!
SOON
HEY, TERENCE.
SLAM
'M GONNA BE IN MY ROOM
WAS IT THE HAT?
WHY, IT MUST BE MAGICAL OR SOMETHING!
NOT MUCH LATER...
I KNOW I SAW IT IN HERE SOMEWHERE...
HERE IT IS!
Terence's Piggybank!
BDUMP BDUMP
BONK
BDUMP BDUMP
OHMIGOD!

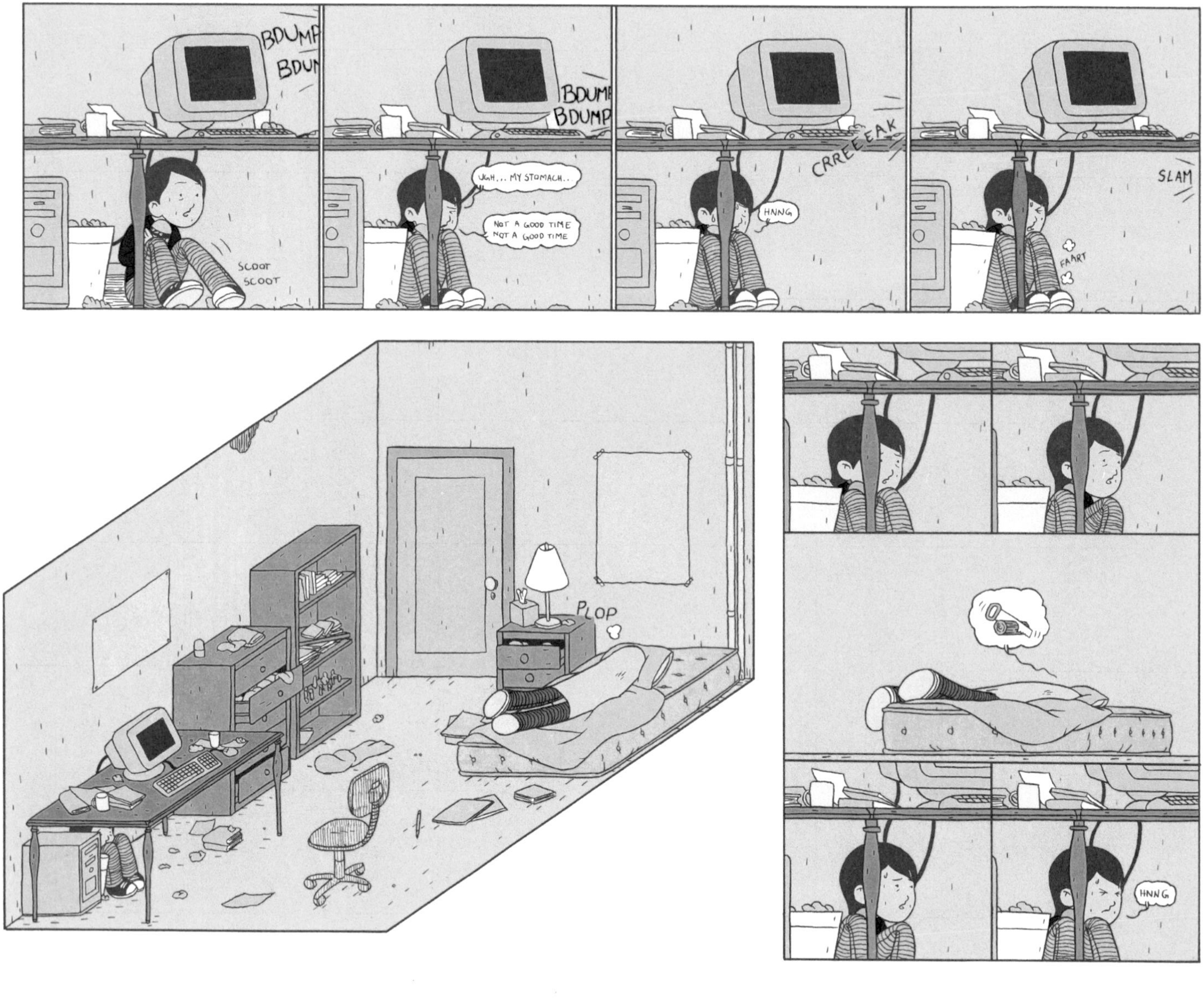
BDUMP
BDUMP
SCOOT
SCOOT
BDUMP
BDUMP
UGH... MY STOMACH...
NOT A GOOD TIME
NOT A GOOD TIME
CRREEEAK
HNNG
SLAM
FAART
PLOP
HNNG

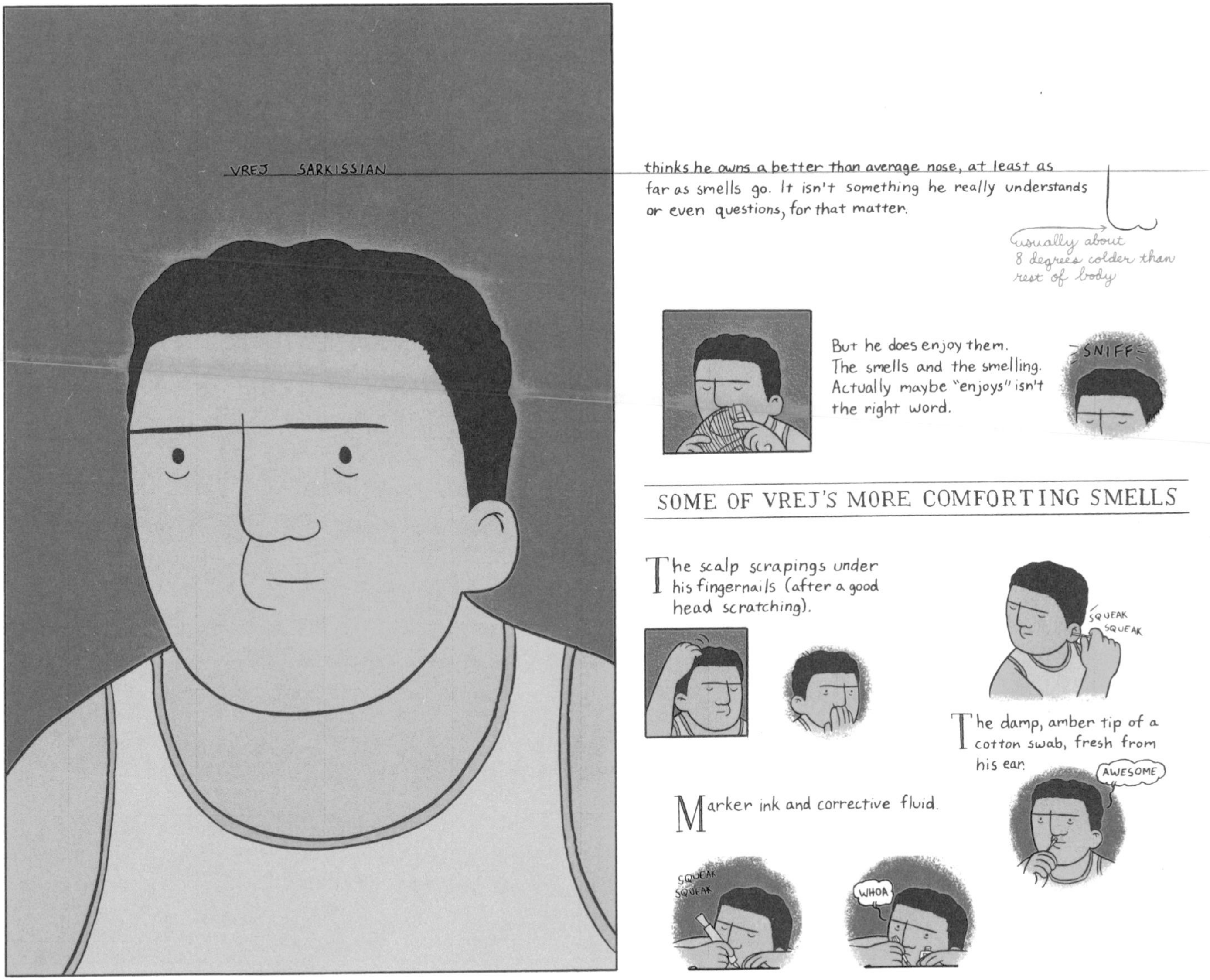
VREJ SARKISSIAN thinks he owns a better than average nose, at least as far as smells go. It isn't something he really understands or even questions, for that matter.
usually about 8 degrees colder than rest of body
But he does enjoy them. The smells and the smelling. Actually maybe "enjoys" isn't the right word.
SNIFF
SOME OF VREJ'S MORE COMFORTING SMELLS
The scalp scrapings under his fingernails (after a good head scratching).
SQUEAK SQUEAK
The damp, amber tip of a cotton swab, fresh from his ear.
AWESOME
Marker ink and corrective fluid.
SQUEAK SQUEAK
WHOA

ALSO:

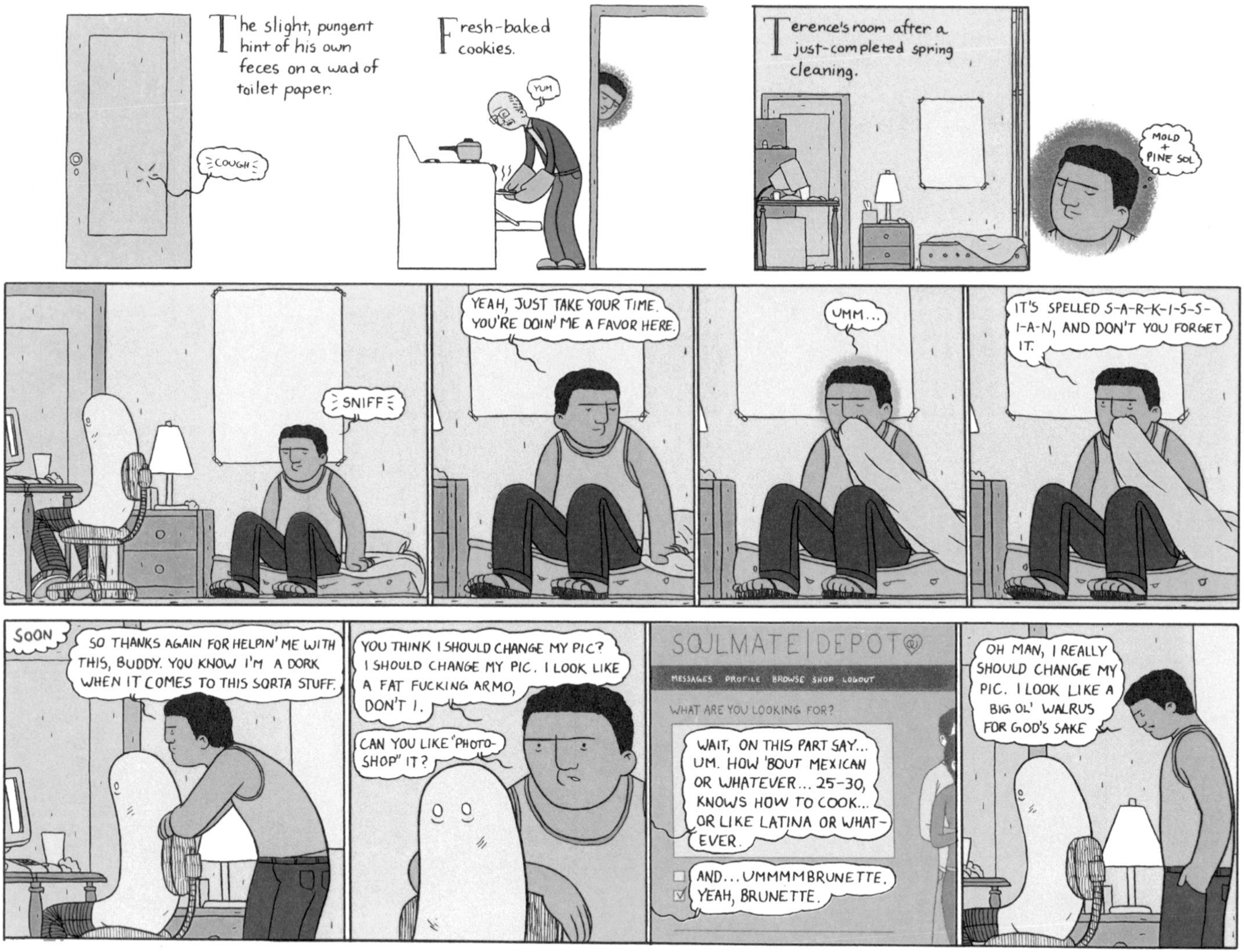
The slight, pungent hint of his own feces on a wad of toilet paper.
COUGH
Fresh-baked cookies.
YUM
Terence's room after a just-completed spring cleaning.
MOLD + PINE SOL
SNIFF
YEAH, JUST TAKE YOUR TIME. YOU'RE DOIN' ME A FAVOR HERE.
UMM...
IT'S SPELLED S-A-R-K-I-S-S-I-A-N, AND DON'T YOU FORGET IT.
SOON
SO THANKS AGAIN FOR HELPIN' ME WITH THIS, BUDDY. YOU KNOW I'M A DORK WHEN IT COMES TO THIS SORTA STUFF.
YOU THINK I SHOULD CHANGE MY PIC? I SHOULD CHANGE MY PIC. I LOOK LIKE A FAT FUCKING ARMO, DON'T I.
CAN YOU LIKE "PHOTO-SHOP" IT?
SOULMATE | DEPOT
MESSAGES PROFILE BROWSE SHOP LOGOUT
WHAT ARE YOU LOOKING FOR?
WAIT, ON THIS PART SAY... UM. HOW 'BOUT MEXICAN OR WHATEVER... 25-30, KNOWS HOW TO COOK... OR LIKE LATINA OR WHAT-EVER.
AND... UMMMMBRUNETTE. YEAH, BRUNETTE.
OH MAN, I REALLY SHOULD CHANGE MY PIC. I LOOK LIKE A BIG OL' WALRUS FOR GOD'S SAKE

AND ALSO, ADDITIONALLY, THE 4 MOST NOTEWORTHY SMELLS THAT INSPIRE A SENSE OF WELL-BEING IN VREJ:

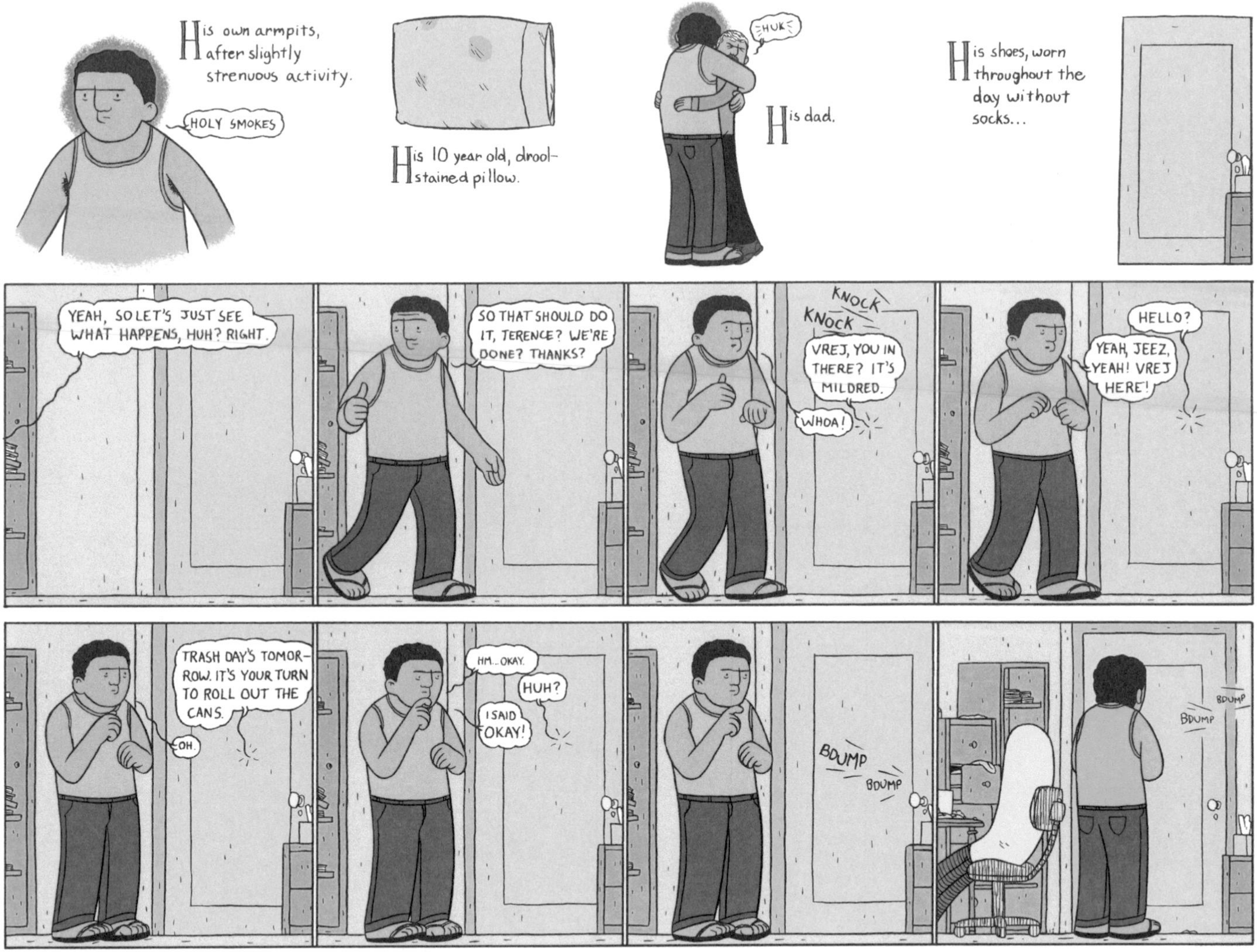

His own armpits, after slightly strenuous activity.
HOLY SMOKES
His 10 year old, drool-stained pillow.
HUK
His dad.
His shoes, worn throughout the day without socks...
YEAH, SO LET'S JUST SEE WHAT HAPPENS, HUH? RIGHT.
SO THAT SHOULD DO IT, TERENCE? WE'RE DONE? THANKS?
KNOCK
KNOCK
VREJ, YOU IN THERE? IT'S MILDRED.
WHOA!
HELLO?
YEAH, JEEZ, YEAH! VREJ HERE!
TRASH DAY'S TOMORROW. IT'S YOUR TURN TO ROLL OUT THE CANS.
OH.
HM... OKAY.
HUH?
I SAID OKAY!
BDUMP
BDUMP
BDUMP
BDUMP

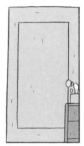

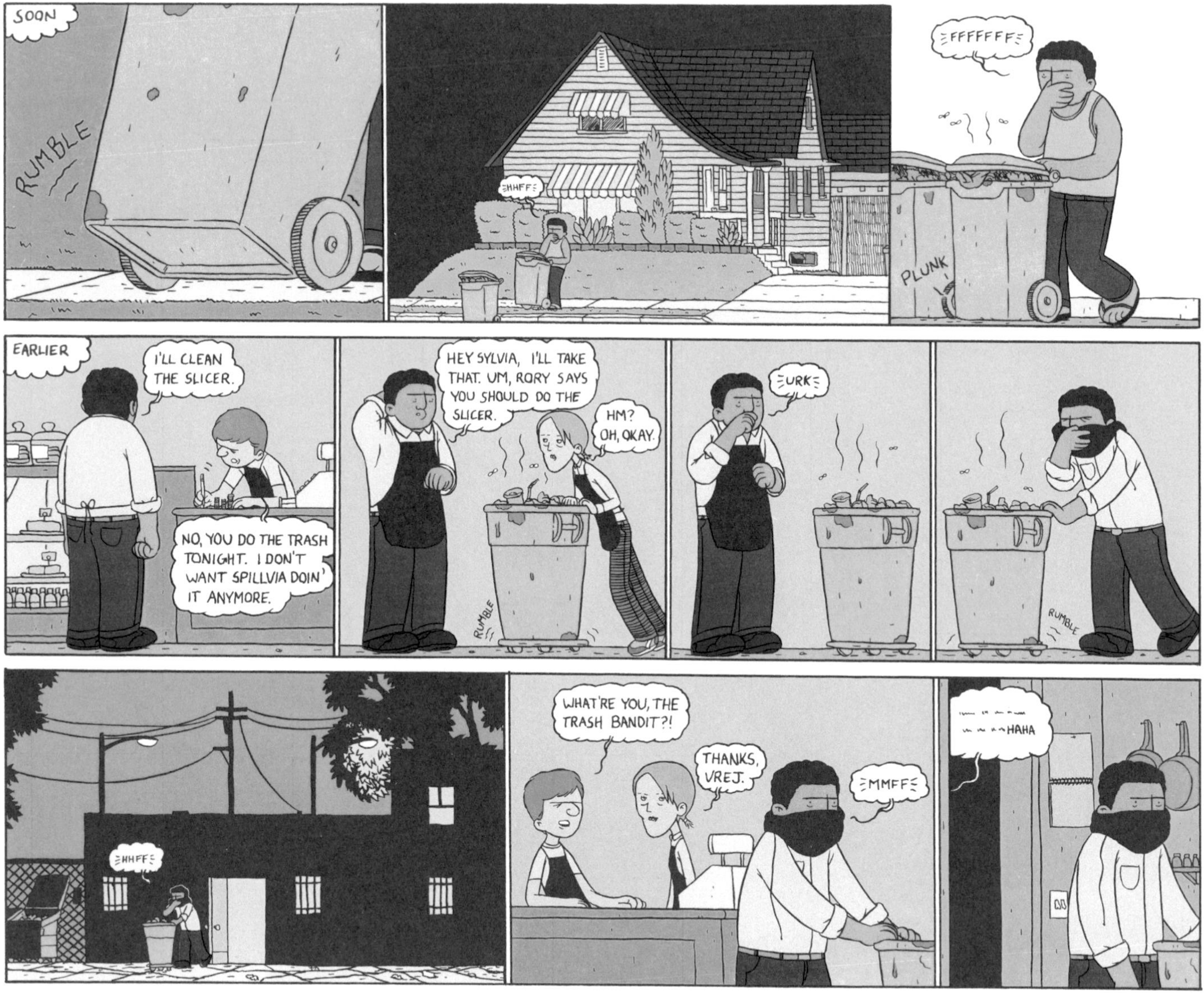
SOON
RUMBLE
HHFF
FFFFFFF
PLUNK
EARLIER
I'LL CLEAN THE SLICER.
NO, YOU DO THE TRASH TONIGHT. I DON'T WANT SPILLVIA DOIN' IT ANYMORE.
HEY SYLVIA, I'LL TAKE THAT. UM, RORY SAYS YOU SHOULD DO THE SLICER.
HM? OH, OKAY.
RUMBLE
URK
RUMBLE
HHFF
WHAT'RE YOU, THE TRASH BANDIT?!
THANKS, VREJ.
MMFF
HAHA

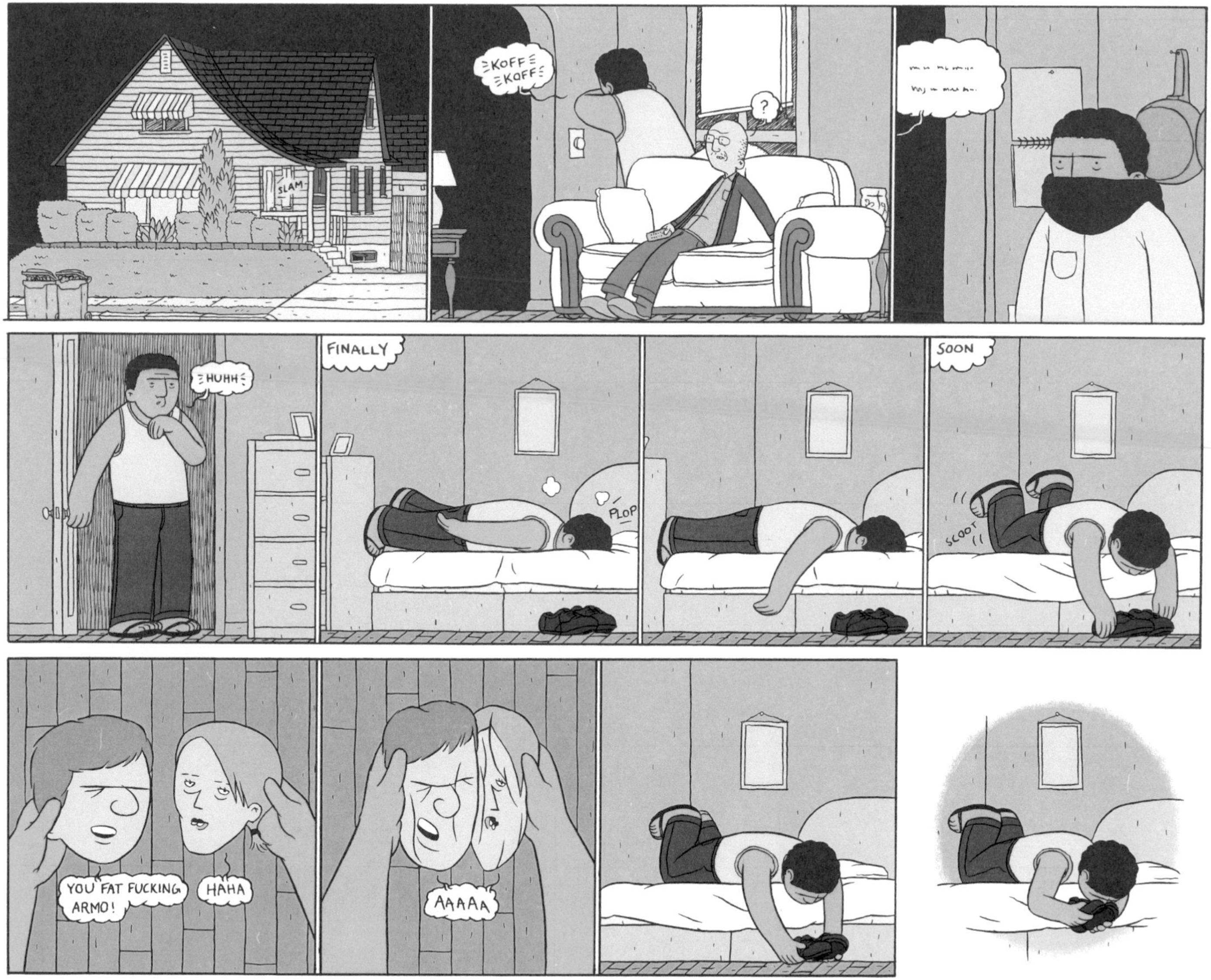
SLAM
KOFF KOFF
?
HUHH
FINALLY
PLOP
SOON
SCOOT
YOU FAT FUCKING ARMO!
HAHA
AAAAA

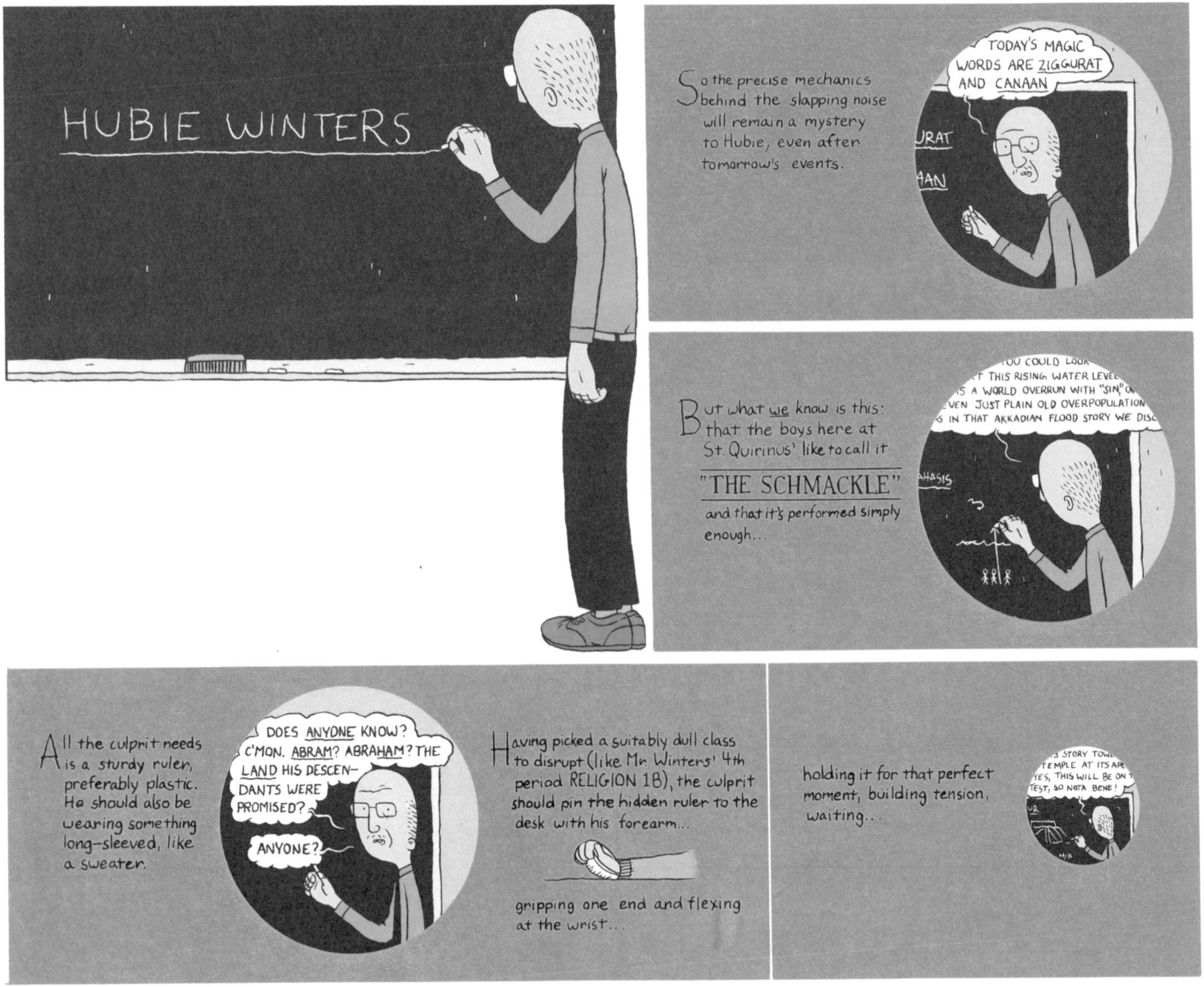
HUBIE WINTERS
So the precise mechanics behind the slapping noise will remain a mystery to Hubie, even after tomorrow's events.
TODAY'S MAGIC WORDS ARE ZIGGURAT AND CANAAN
URAT
AAN
But what we know is this: that the boys here at St. Quirinus' like to call it
"THE SCHMACKLE"
and that it's performed simply enough...
OU COULD LOOK
T THIS RISING WATER LEVE
S A WORLD OVERRUN WITH "SIN," O
VEN JUST PLAIN OLD OVERPOPULATION
S IN THAT AKKADIAN FLOOD STORY WE DISC
AHASIS
All the culprit needs is a sturdy ruler, preferably plastic. He should also be wearing something long-sleeved, like a sweater.
DOES ANYONE KNOW? C'MON. ABRAM? ABRAHAM? THE LAND HIS DESCENDANTS WERE PROMISED?
ANYONE?
Having picked a suitably dull class to disrupt (like Mr. Winters' 4th period RELIGION 1B), the culprit should pin the hidden ruler to the desk with his forearm...
gripping one end and flexing at the wrist...
holding it for that perfect moment, building tension, waiting...
S STORY TOW
TEMPLE AT ITS AP
YES, THIS WILL BE ON
TEST, SO NOTA BENE!
UR

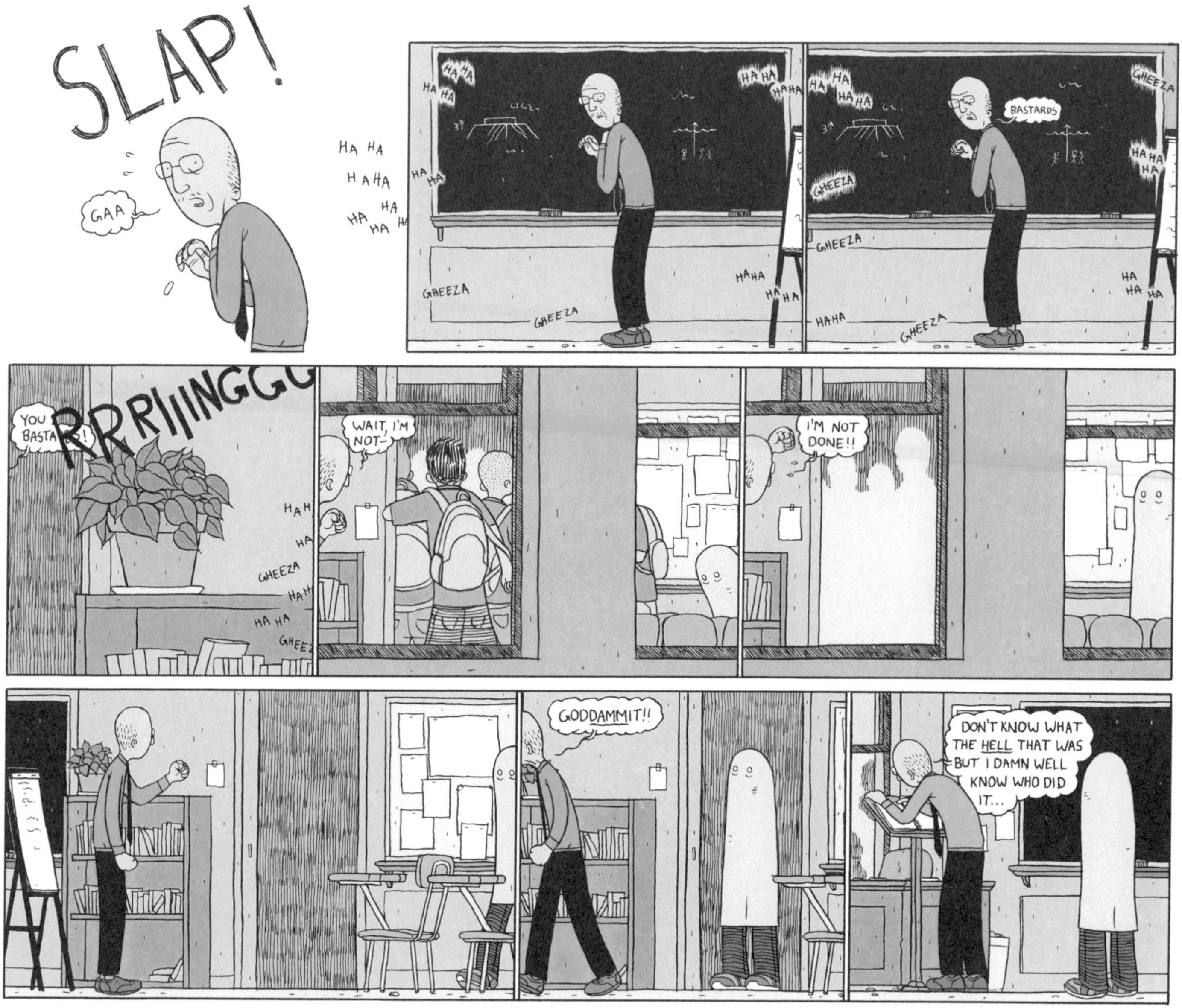
SLAP!
GAA
HA HA
HA HA
HA HA
HA HA HA
HA HA
HA HA HA HA
HA HA HA HA
GHEEZA
GHEEZA
HA HA
HA HA
HA HA HA HA
GHEEZA
GHEEZA
BASTARDS
HA HA HA
GHEEZA
HAHA
GHEEZA
HA HA HA
YOU BASTARDS!
RRRIIINGGG
HA HA
HA
GHEEZA
HA HA
HA HA
GHEEZ
WAIT, I'M NOT–
I'M NOT DONE!!
GODDAMMIT!!
DON'T KNOW WHAT THE HELL THAT WAS BUT I DAMN WELL KNOW WHO DID IT...

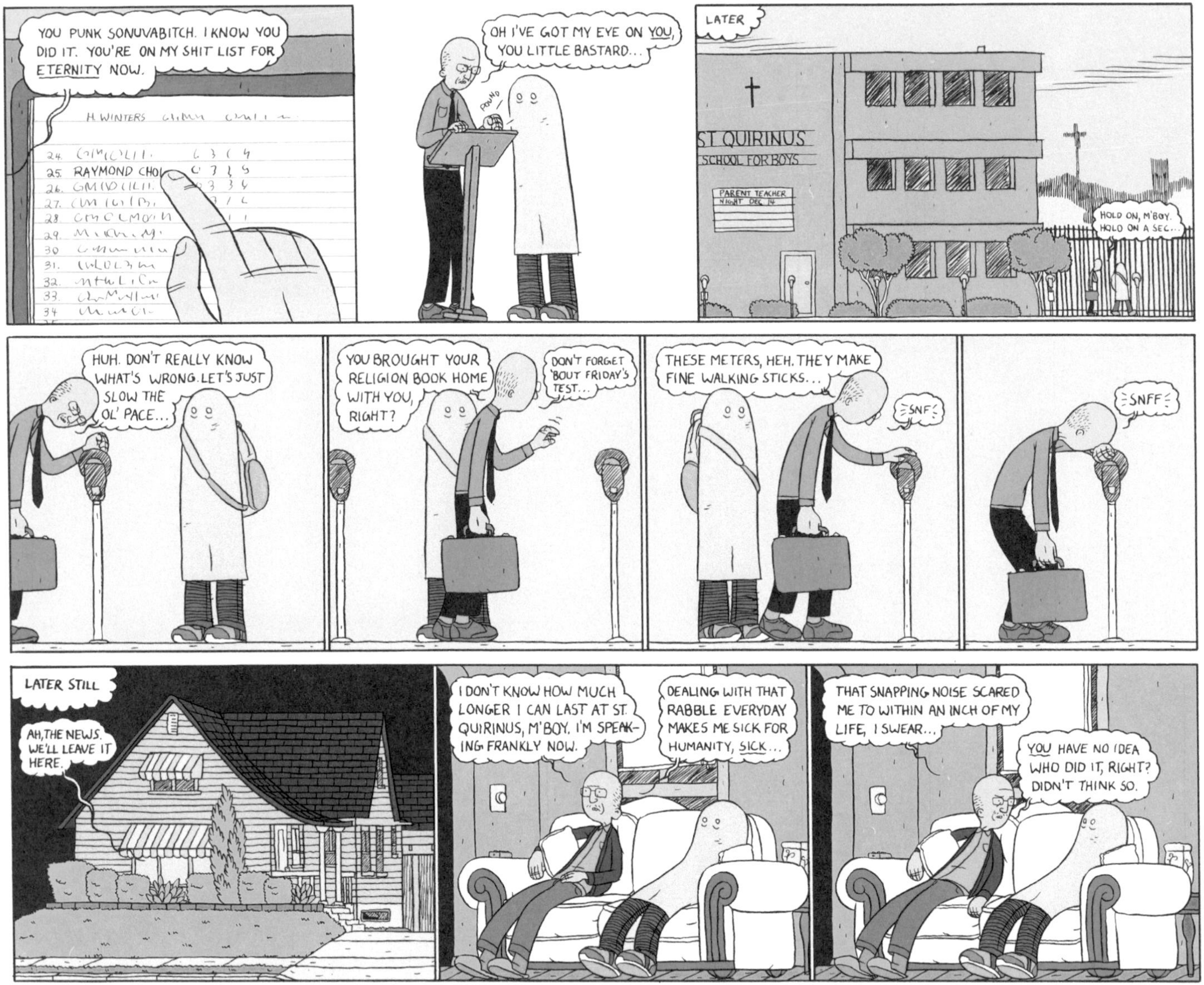
YOU PUNK SONUVABITCH. I KNOW YOU DID IT. YOU'RE ON MY SHIT LIST FOR ETERNITY NOW.
H. WINTERS
25. RAYMOND CHOI
OH I'VE GOT MY EYE ON YOU, YOU LITTLE BASTARD...
POUND
LATER
ST QUIRINUS SCHOOL FOR BOYS
PARENT TEACHER NIGHT DEC 14
HOLD ON, M'BOY. HOLD ON A SEC...
HUH. DON'T REALLY KNOW WHAT'S WRONG. LET'S JUST SLOW THE OL' PACE...
YOU BROUGHT YOUR RELIGION BOOK HOME WITH YOU, RIGHT?
DON'T FORGET 'BOUT FRIDAY'S TEST...
THESE METERS, HEH. THEY MAKE FINE WALKING STICKS...
SNF
SNFF
LATER STILL
AH, THE NEWS. WE'LL LEAVE IT HERE.
I DON'T KNOW HOW MUCH LONGER I CAN LAST AT ST. QUIRINUS, M'BOY. I'M SPEAKING FRANKLY NOW.
DEALING WITH THAT RABBLE EVERYDAY MAKES ME SICK FOR HUMANITY, SICK...
THAT SNAPPING NOISE SCARED ME TO WITHIN AN INCH OF MY LIFE, I SWEAR...
YOU HAVE NO IDEA WHO DID IT, RIGHT? DIDN'T THINK SO.

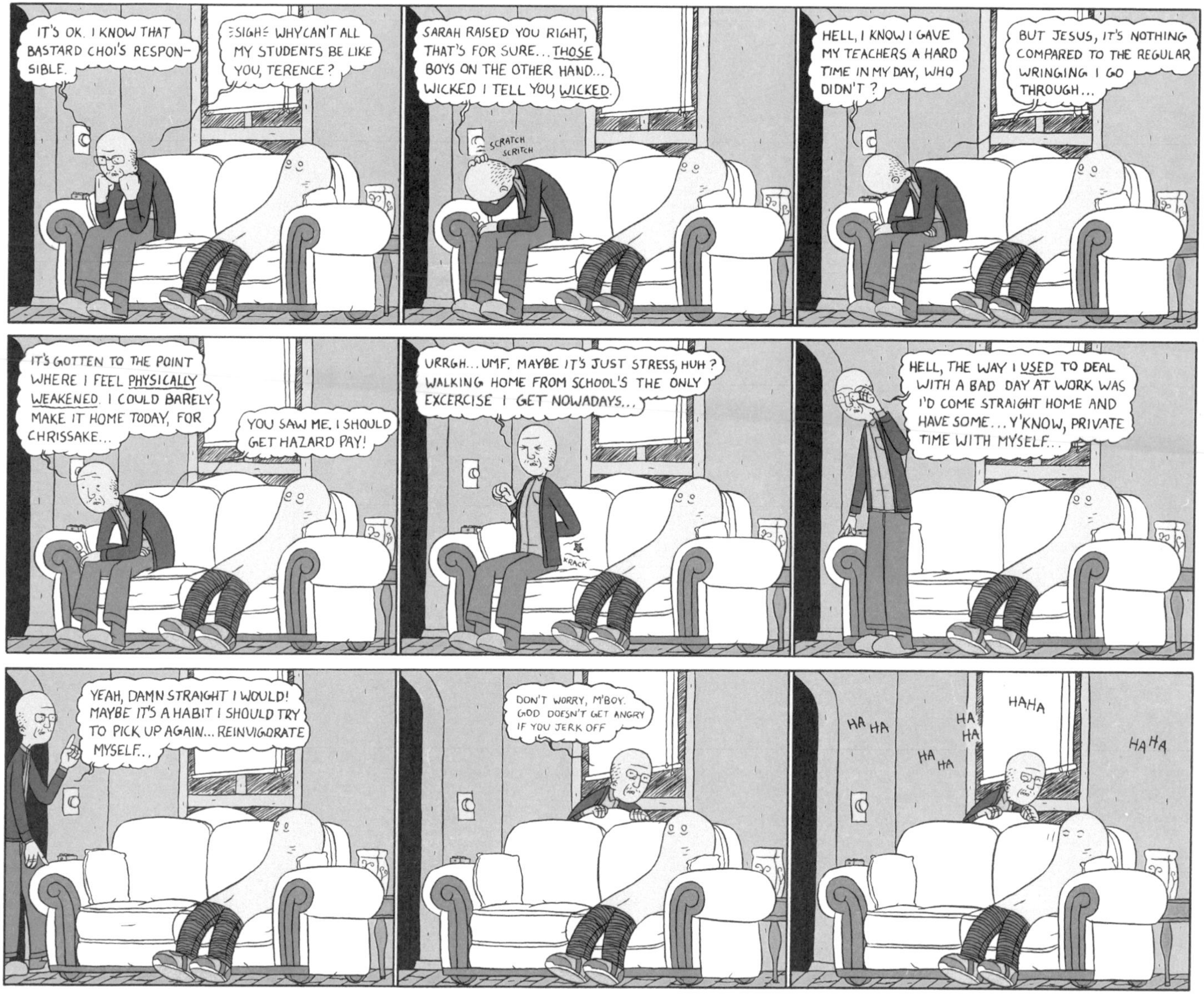
IT'S OK. I KNOW THAT BASTARD CHOI'S RESPONSIBLE.
=SIGH= WHY CAN'T ALL MY STUDENTS BE LIKE YOU, TERENCE?
SARAH RAISED YOU RIGHT, THAT'S FOR SURE... THOSE BOYS ON THE OTHER HAND... WICKED I TELL YOU, WICKED.
SCRATCH SCRITCH
HELL, I KNOW I GAVE MY TEACHERS A HARD TIME IN MY DAY, WHO DIDN'T?
BUT JESUS, IT'S NOTHING COMPARED TO THE REGULAR WRINGING I GO THROUGH...
IT'S GOTTEN TO THE POINT WHERE I FEEL PHYSICALLY WEAKENED. I COULD BARELY MAKE IT HOME TODAY, FOR CHRISSAKE...
YOU SAW ME. I SHOULD GET HAZARD PAY!
URRGH... UMF. MAYBE IT'S JUST STRESS, HUH? WALKING HOME FROM SCHOOL'S THE ONLY EXCERCISE I GET NOWADAYS...
KRACK
HELL, THE WAY I USED TO DEAL WITH A BAD DAY AT WORK WAS I'D COME STRAIGHT HOME AND HAVE SOME... Y'KNOW, PRIVATE TIME WITH MYSELF...
YEAH, DAMN STRAIGHT I WOULD! MAYBE IT'S A HABIT I SHOULD TRY TO PICK UP AGAIN... REINVIGORATE MYSELF...
DON'T WORRY, M'BOY. GOD DOESN'T GET ANGRY IF YOU JERK OFF
HA HA
HA HA
HA HA
HAHA
HA HA

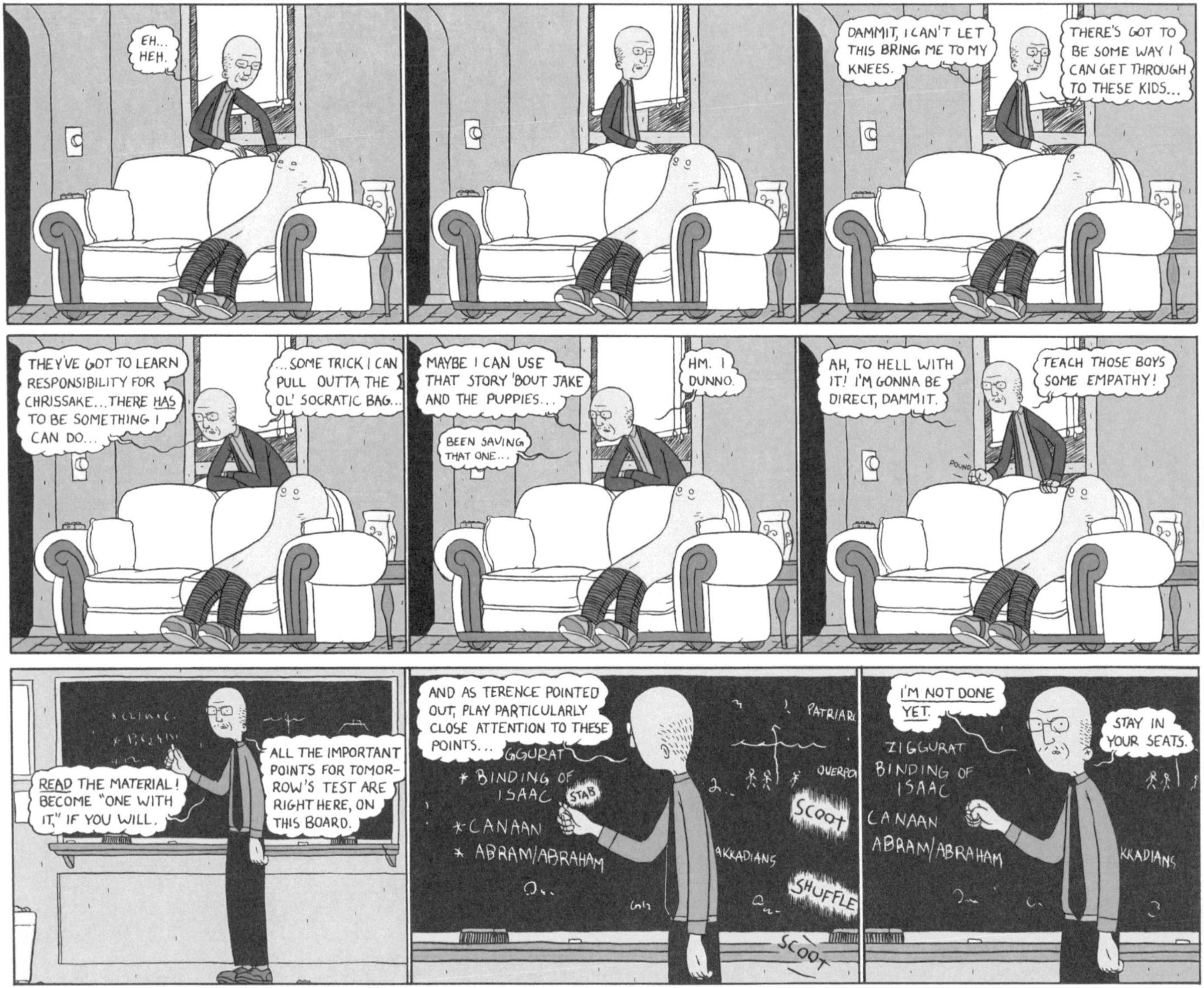
EH... HEH.
DAMMIT, I CAN'T LET THIS BRING ME TO MY KNEES.
THERE'S GOT TO BE SOME WAY I CAN GET THROUGH TO THESE KIDS...
THEY'VE GOT TO LEARN RESPONSIBILITY FOR CHRISSAKE... THERE HAS TO BE SOMETHING I CAN DO...
...SOME TRICK I CAN PULL OUTTA THE OL' SOCRATIC BAG...
MAYBE I CAN USE THAT STORY 'BOUT JAKE AND THE PUPPIES...
BEEN SAVING THAT ONE...
HM. I DUNNO.
AH, TO HELL WITH IT! I'M GONNA BE DIRECT, DAMMIT.
POUND
TEACH THOSE BOYS SOME EMPATHY!
READ THE MATERIAL! BECOME "ONE WITH IT," IF YOU WILL.
ALL THE IMPORTANT POINTS FOR TOMORROW'S TEST ARE RIGHT HERE, ON THIS BOARD.
AND AS TERENCE POINTED OUT, PLAY PARTICULARLY CLOSE ATTENTION TO THESE POINTS...
STAB
SCOOT
SHUFFLE
SCOOT
I'M NOT DONE YET.
STAY IN YOUR SEATS.
ZIGGURAT
BINDING OF ISAAC
CANAAN
ABRAM/ABRAHAM

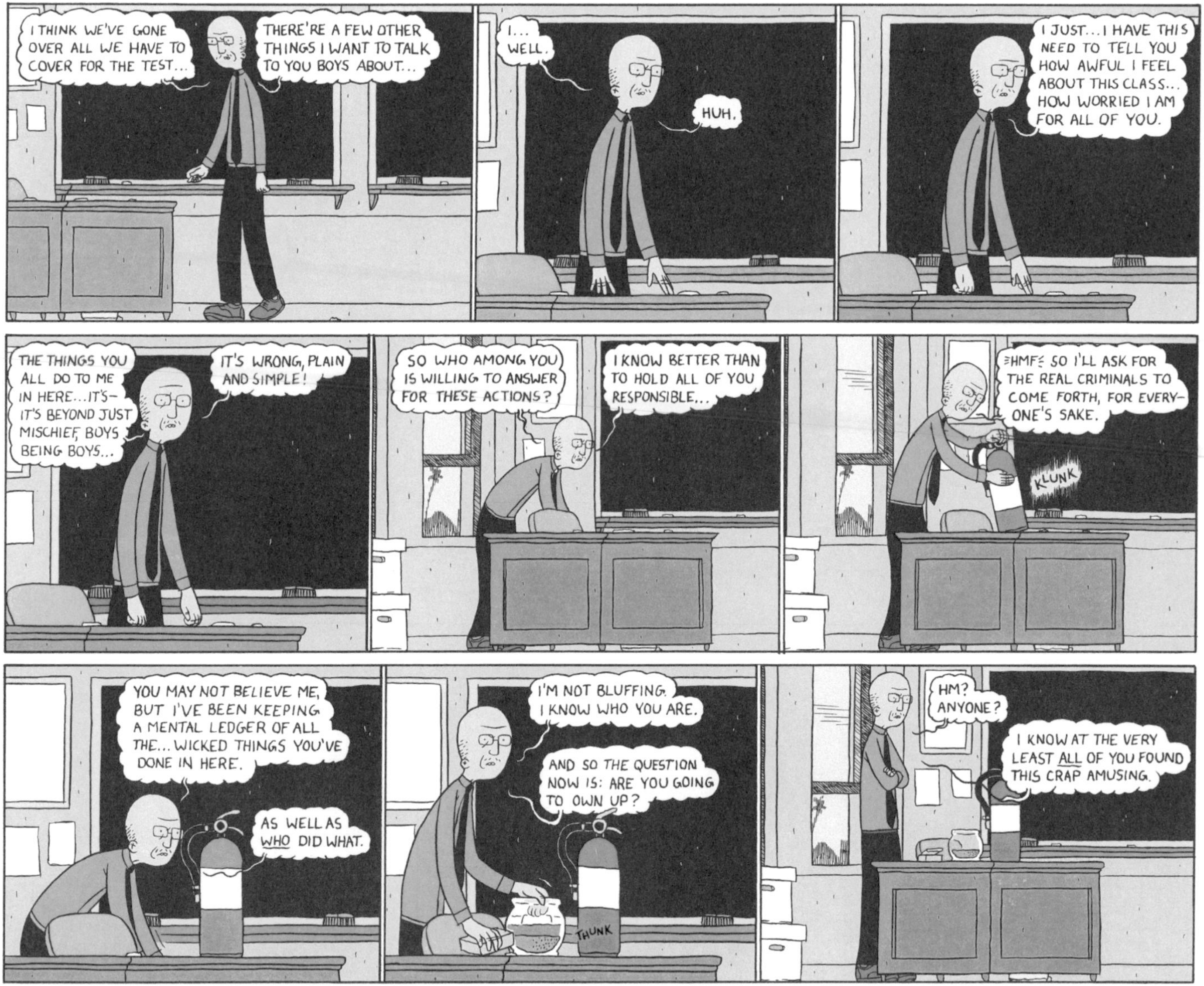
I THINK WE'VE GONE OVER ALL WE HAVE TO COVER FOR THE TEST...
THERE'RE A FEW OTHER THINGS I WANT TO TALK TO YOU BOYS ABOUT...
I... WELL.
HUH.
I JUST... I HAVE THIS NEED TO TELL YOU HOW AWFUL I FEEL ABOUT THIS CLASS... HOW WORRIED I AM FOR ALL OF YOU.
THE THINGS YOU ALL DO TO ME IN HERE... IT'S— IT'S BEYOND JUST MISCHIEF, BOYS BEING BOYS...
IT'S WRONG, PLAIN AND SIMPLE!
SO WHO AMONG YOU IS WILLING TO ANSWER FOR THESE ACTIONS?
I KNOW BETTER THAN TO HOLD ALL OF YOU RESPONSIBLE...
HMF SO I'LL ASK FOR THE REAL CRIMINALS TO COME FORTH, FOR EVERY-ONE'S SAKE.
KLUNK
YOU MAY NOT BELIEVE ME, BUT I'VE BEEN KEEPING A MENTAL LEDGER OF ALL THE... WICKED THINGS YOU'VE DONE IN HERE.
AS WELL AS WHO DID WHAT.
I'M NOT BLUFFING. I KNOW WHO YOU ARE.
AND SO THE QUESTION NOW IS: ARE YOU GOING TO OWN UP?
THUNK
HM? ANYONE?
I KNOW AT THE VERY LEAST ALL OF YOU FOUND THIS CRAP AMUSING.

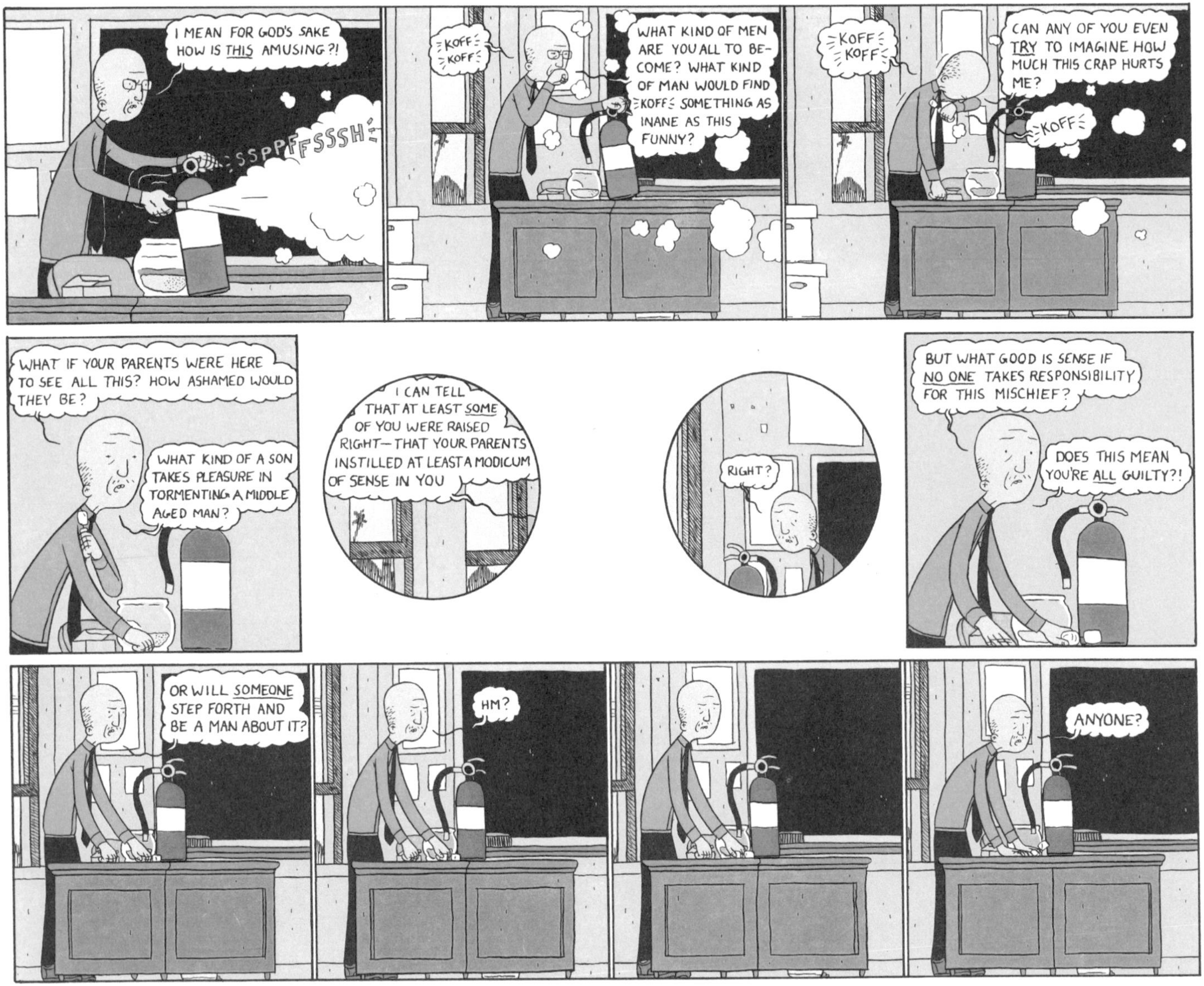
I MEAN FOR GOD'S SAKE HOW IS THIS AMUSING?!
SSPPFFSSSH
KOFF KOFF
WHAT KIND OF MEN ARE YOU ALL TO BE- COME? WHAT KIND OF MAN WOULD FIND KOFF SOMETHING AS INANE AS THIS FUNNY?
KOFF KOFF
CAN ANY OF YOU EVEN TRY TO IMAGINE HOW MUCH THIS CRAP HURTS ME?
KOFF
WHAT IF YOUR PARENTS WERE HERE TO SEE ALL THIS? HOW ASHAMED WOULD THEY BE?
WHAT KIND OF A SON TAKES PLEASURE IN TORMENTING A MIDDLE AGED MAN?
I CAN TELL THAT AT LEAST SOME OF YOU WERE RAISED RIGHT—THAT YOUR PARENTS INSTILLED AT LEAST A MODICUM OF SENSE IN YOU
RIGHT?
BUT WHAT GOOD IS SENSE IF NO ONE TAKES RESPONSIBILITY FOR THIS MISCHIEF?
DOES THIS MEAN YOU'RE ALL GUILTY?!
OR WILL SOMEONE STEP FORTH AND BE A MAN ABOUT IT?
HM?
ANYONE?

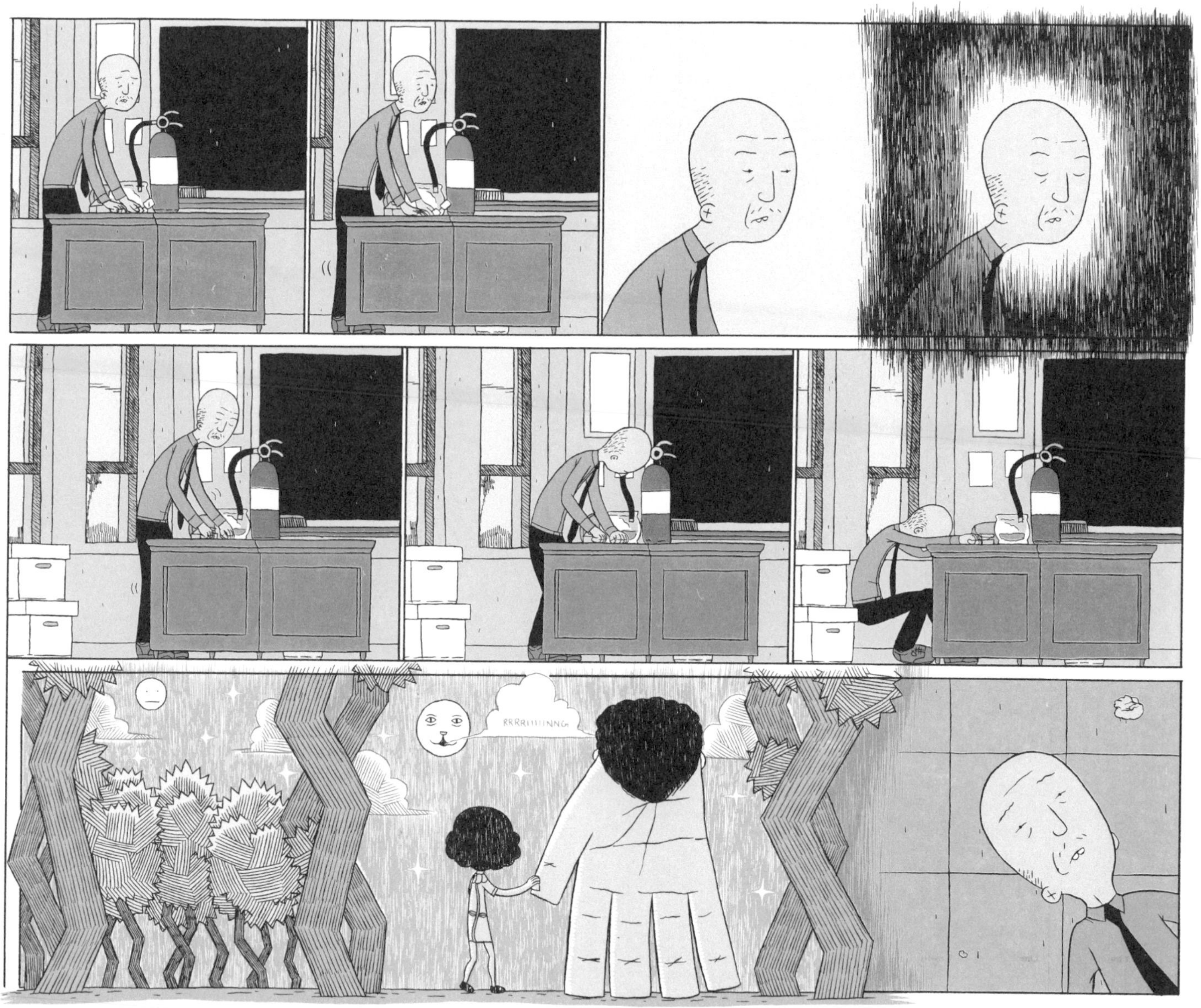
RRRRIIIIIINNG

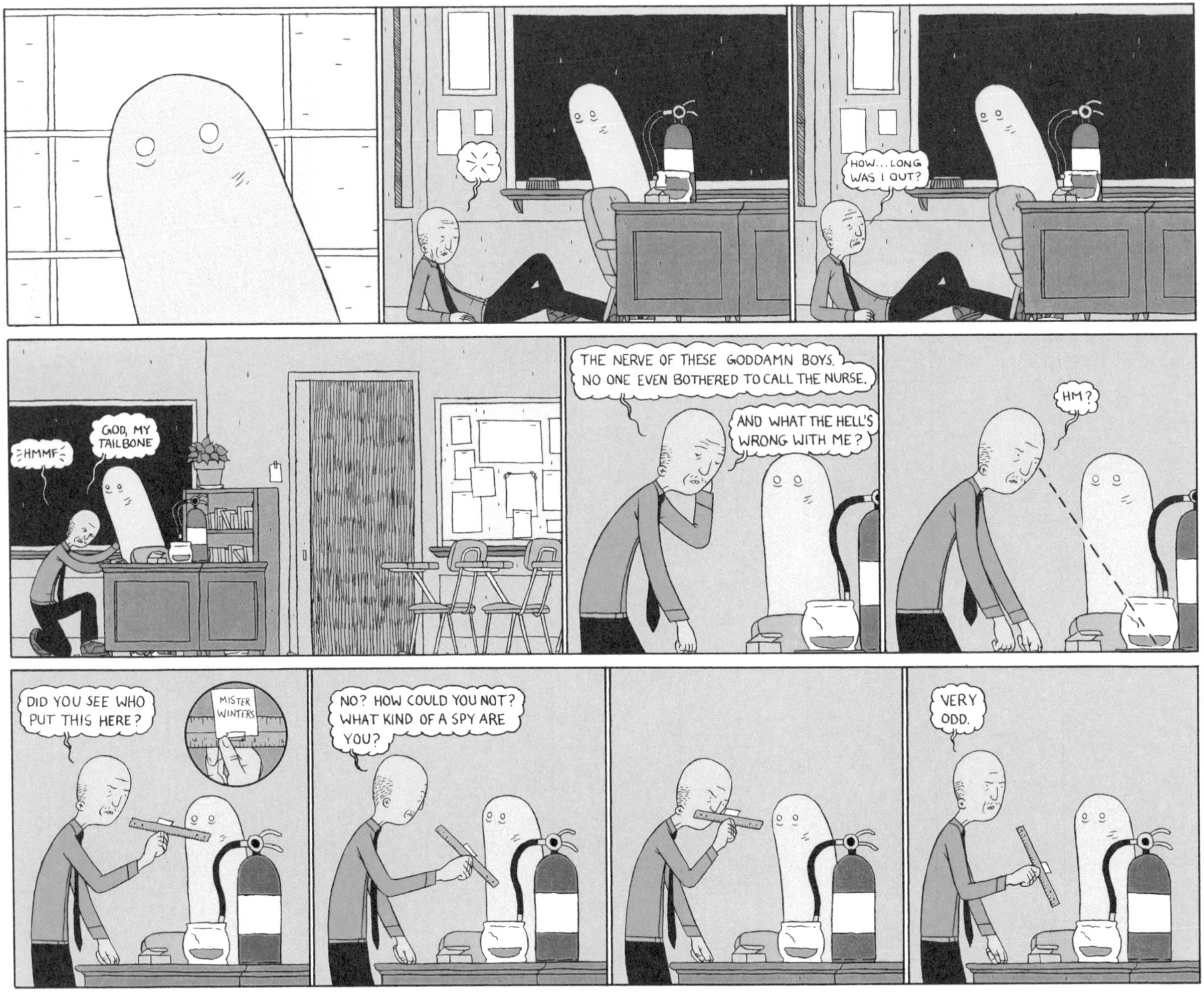
HOW... LONG WAS I OUT?
HMMF
GOD, MY TAILBONE
THE NERVE OF THESE GODDAMN BOYS. NO ONE EVEN BOTHERED TO CALL THE NURSE.
AND WHAT THE HELL'S WRONG WITH ME?
HM?
DID YOU SEE WHO PUT THIS HERE?
MISTER WINTERS
NO? HOW COULD YOU NOT? WHAT KIND OF A SPY ARE YOU?
VERY ODD.

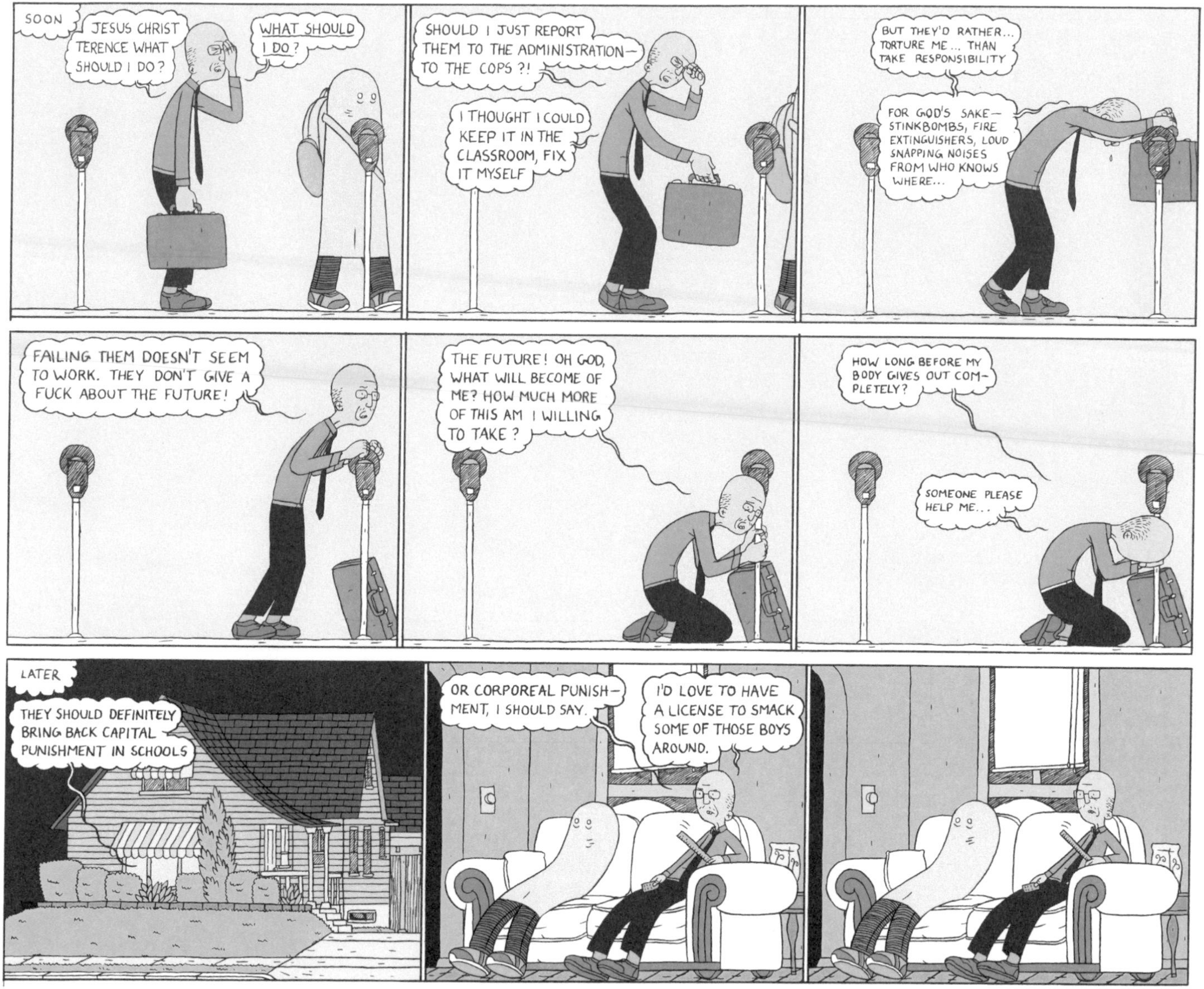
SOON
JESUS CHRIST TERENCE WHAT SHOULD I DO?
WHAT SHOULD I DO?
SHOULD I JUST REPORT THEM TO THE ADMINISTRATION— TO THE COPS?!
I THOUGHT I COULD KEEP IT IN THE CLASSROOM, FIX IT MYSELF
BUT THEY'D RATHER... TORTURE ME... THAN TAKE RESPONSIBILITY
FOR GOD'S SAKE— STINKBOMBS, FIRE EXTINGUISHERS, LOUD SNAPPING NOISES FROM WHO KNOWS WHERE...
FAILING THEM DOESN'T SEEM TO WORK. THEY DON'T GIVE A FUCK ABOUT THE FUTURE!
THE FUTURE! OH GOD, WHAT WILL BECOME OF ME? HOW MUCH MORE OF THIS AM I WILLING TO TAKE?
HOW LONG BEFORE MY BODY GIVES OUT COMPLETELY?
SOMEONE PLEASE HELP ME...
LATER
THEY SHOULD DEFINITELY BRING BACK CAPITAL PUNISHMENT IN SCHOOLS
OR CORPOREAL PUNISHMENT, I SHOULD SAY.
I'D LOVE TO HAVE A LICENSE TO SMACK SOME OF THOSE BOYS AROUND.

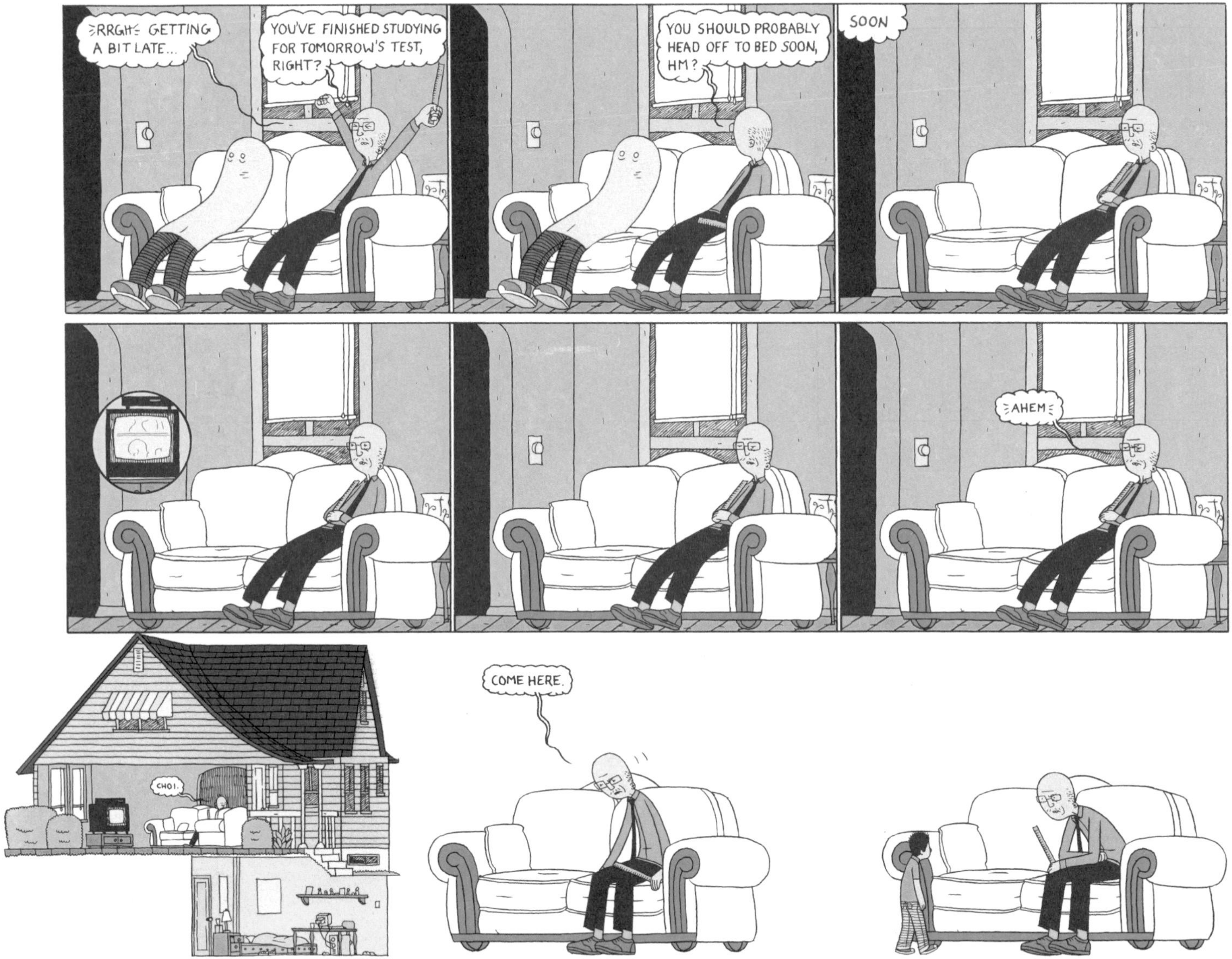

≷RRGH≶ GETTING A BIT LATE...
YOU'VE FINISHED STUDYING FOR TOMORROW'S TEST, RIGHT?
YOU SHOULD PROBABLY HEAD OFF TO BED SOON, HM?
SOON
≷AHEM≶
CHOI.
COME HERE.

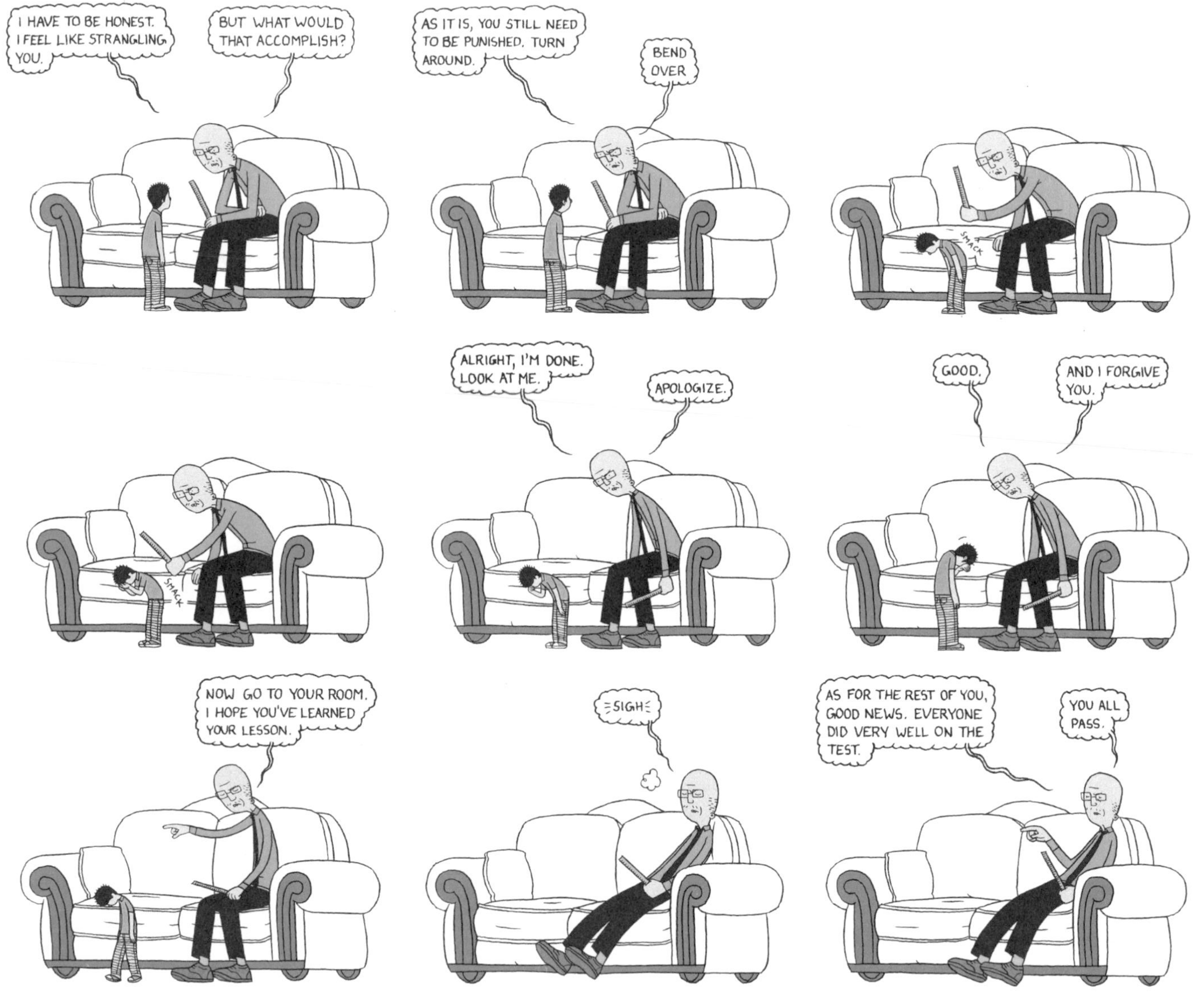
I HAVE TO BE HONEST. I FEEL LIKE STRANGLING YOU.
BUT WHAT WOULD THAT ACCOMPLISH?
AS IT IS, YOU STILL NEED TO BE PUNISHED. TURN AROUND.
BEND OVER
SMACK
SMACK
ALRIGHT, I'M DONE. LOOK AT ME.
APOLOGIZE.
GOOD.
AND I FORGIVE YOU.
NOW GO TO YOUR ROOM. I HOPE YOU'VE LEARNED YOUR LESSON.
SIGH
AS FOR THE REST OF YOU, GOOD NEWS. EVERYONE DID VERY WELL ON THE TEST.
YOU ALL PASS.

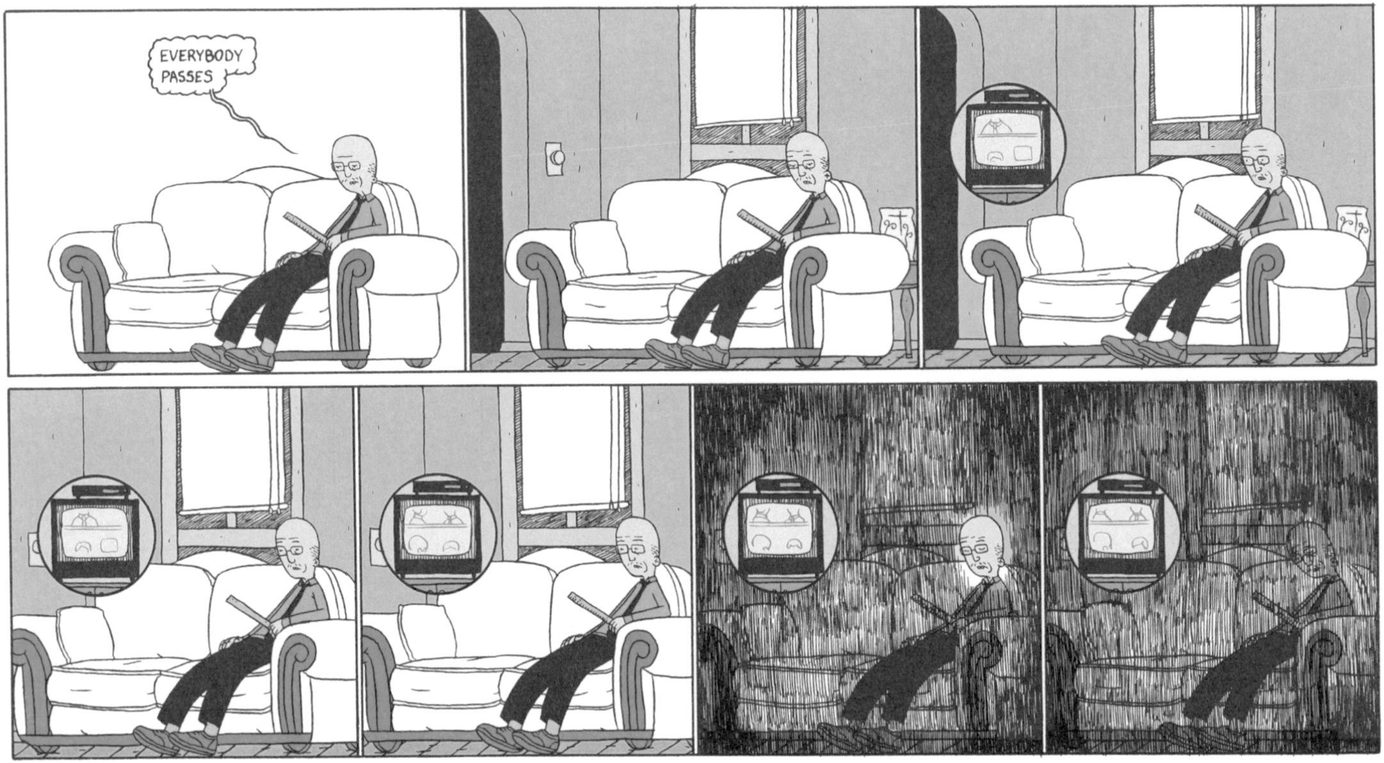
EVERYBODY PASSES

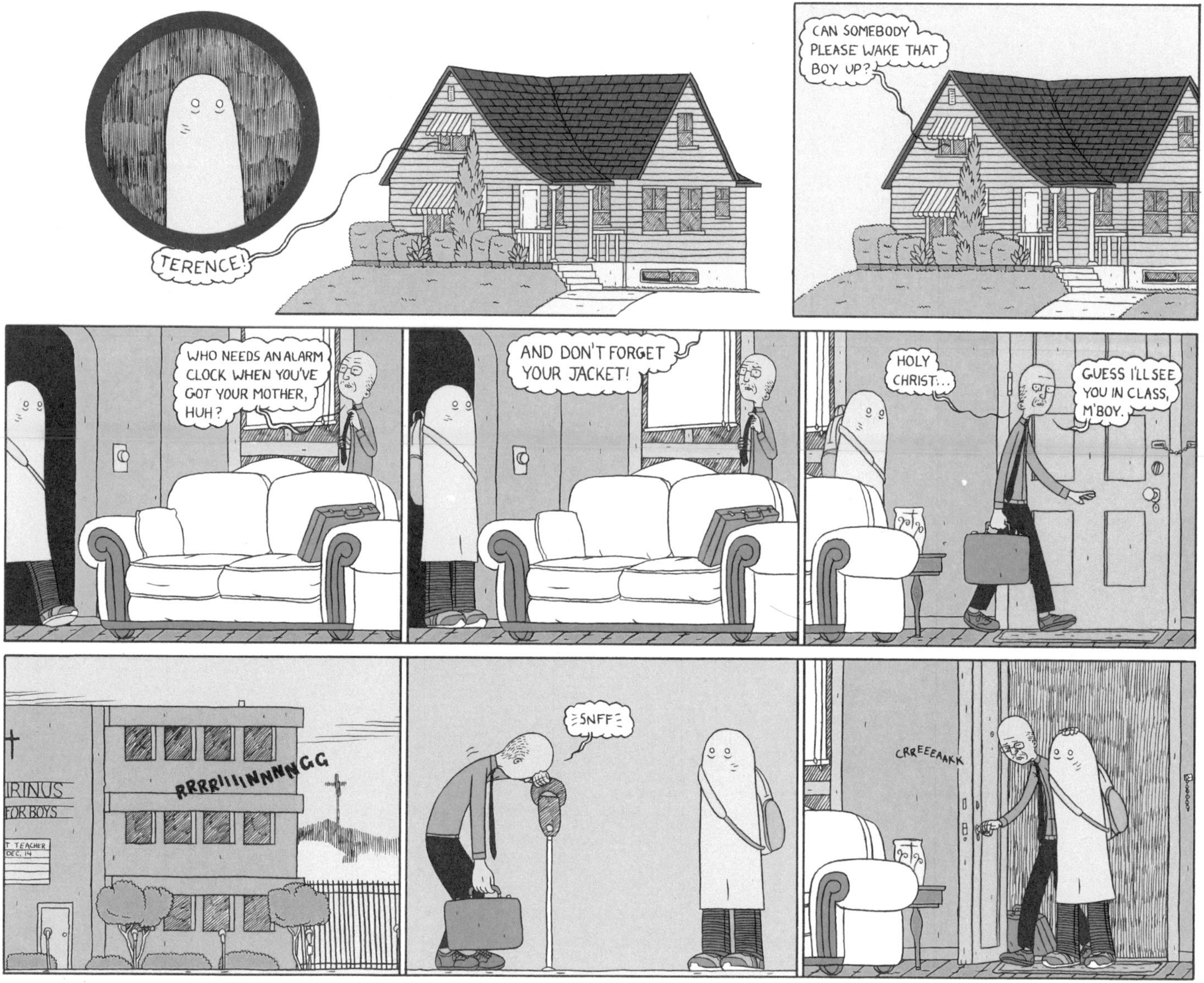
TERENCE!
CAN SOMEBODY PLEASE WAKE THAT BOY UP?
WHO NEEDS AN ALARM CLOCK WHEN YOU'VE GOT YOUR MOTHER, HUH?
AND DON'T FORGET YOUR JACKET!
HOLY CHRIST...
GUESS I'LL SEE YOU IN CLASS, M'BOY.
IRINUS
FOR BOYS
T TEACHER
DEC. 14
RRRRIIIIINNNNGG
SNFF
CRREEEEAAKK

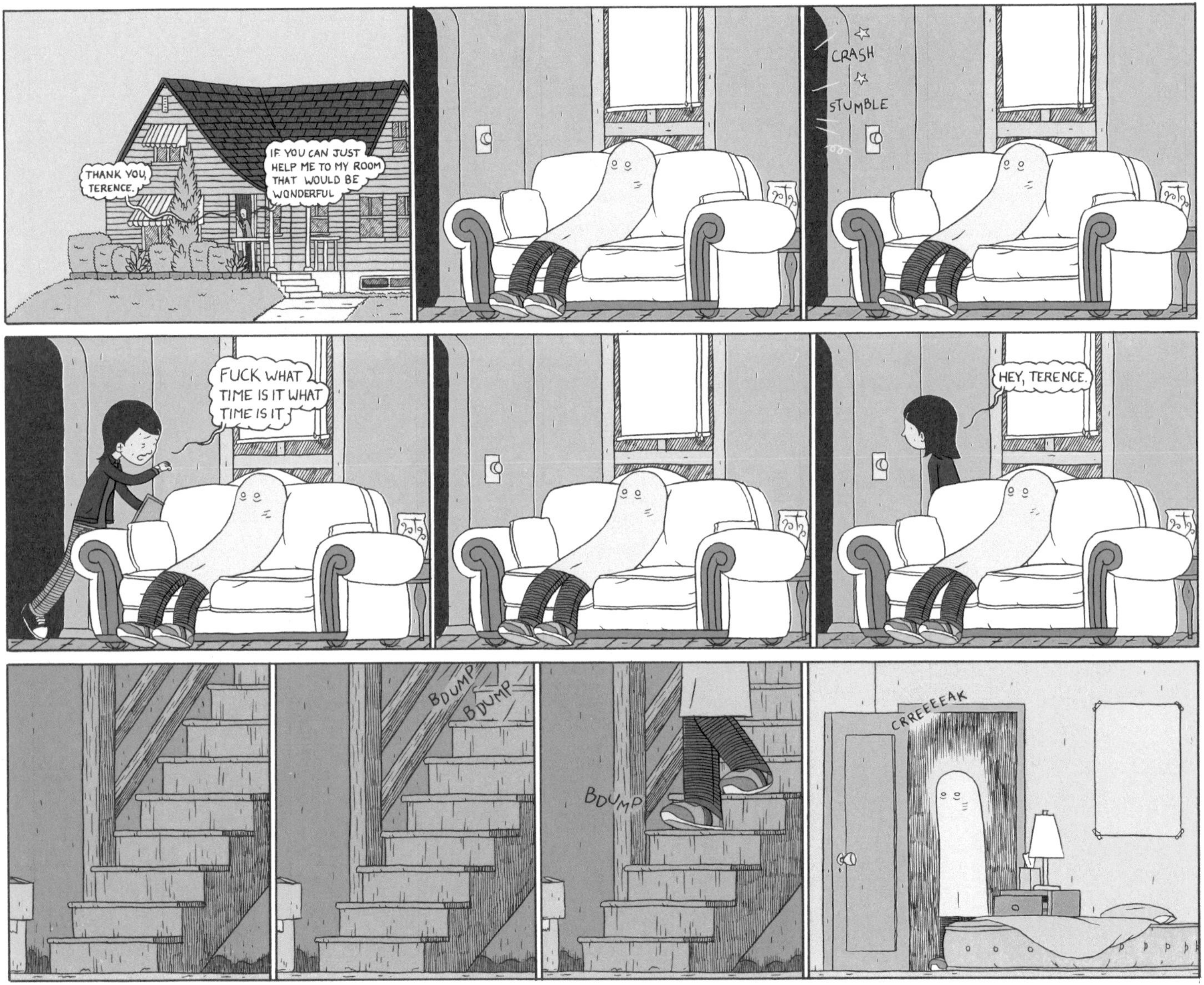
THANK YOU, TERENCE.
IF YOU CAN JUST HELP ME TO MY ROOM THAT WOULD BE WONDERFUL
CRASH
STUMBLE
FUCK WHAT TIME IS IT WHAT TIME IS IT
HEY, TERENCE.
BDUMP
BDUMP
BDUMP
CRREEEEAK

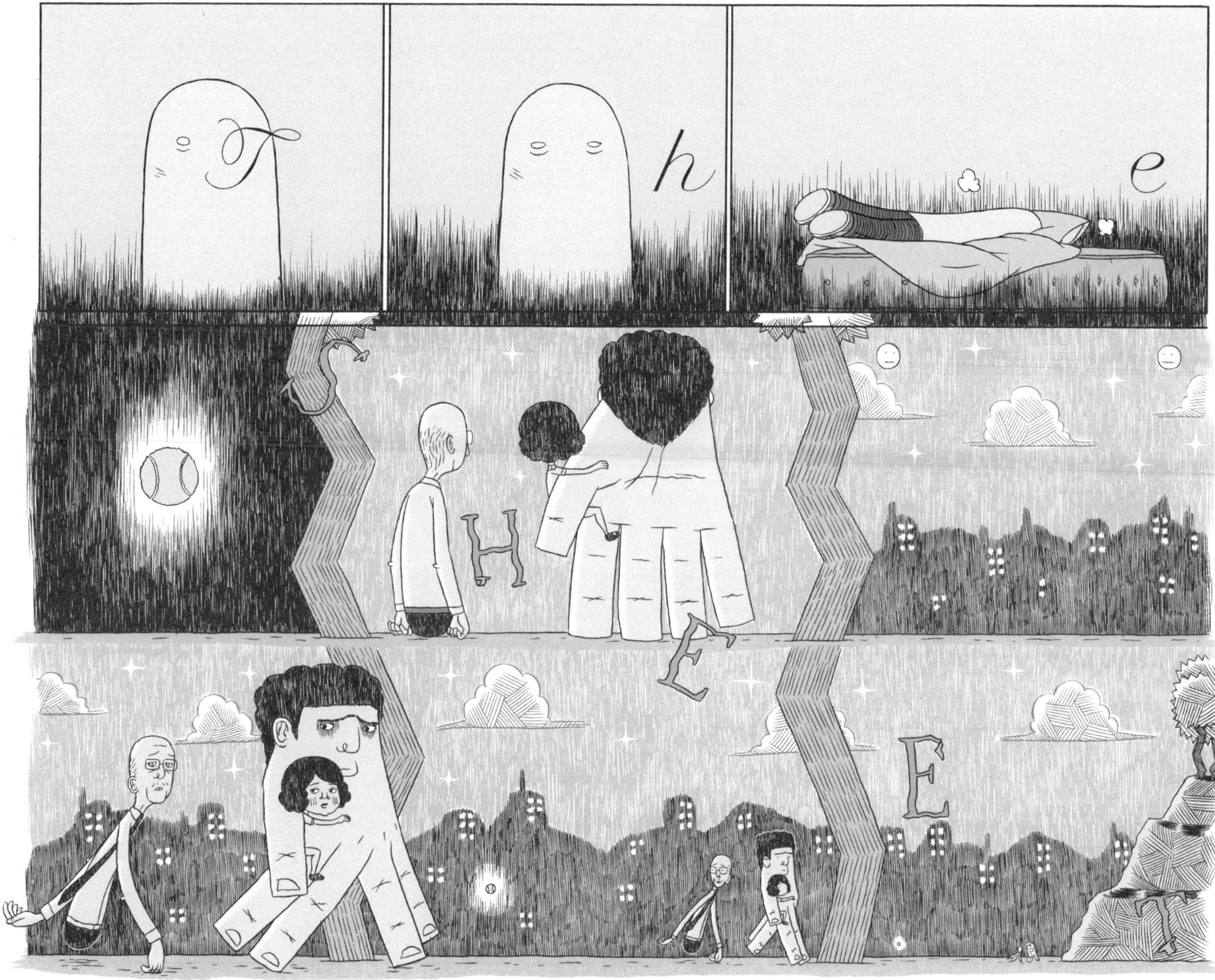
T
h
e
H
E
E
T

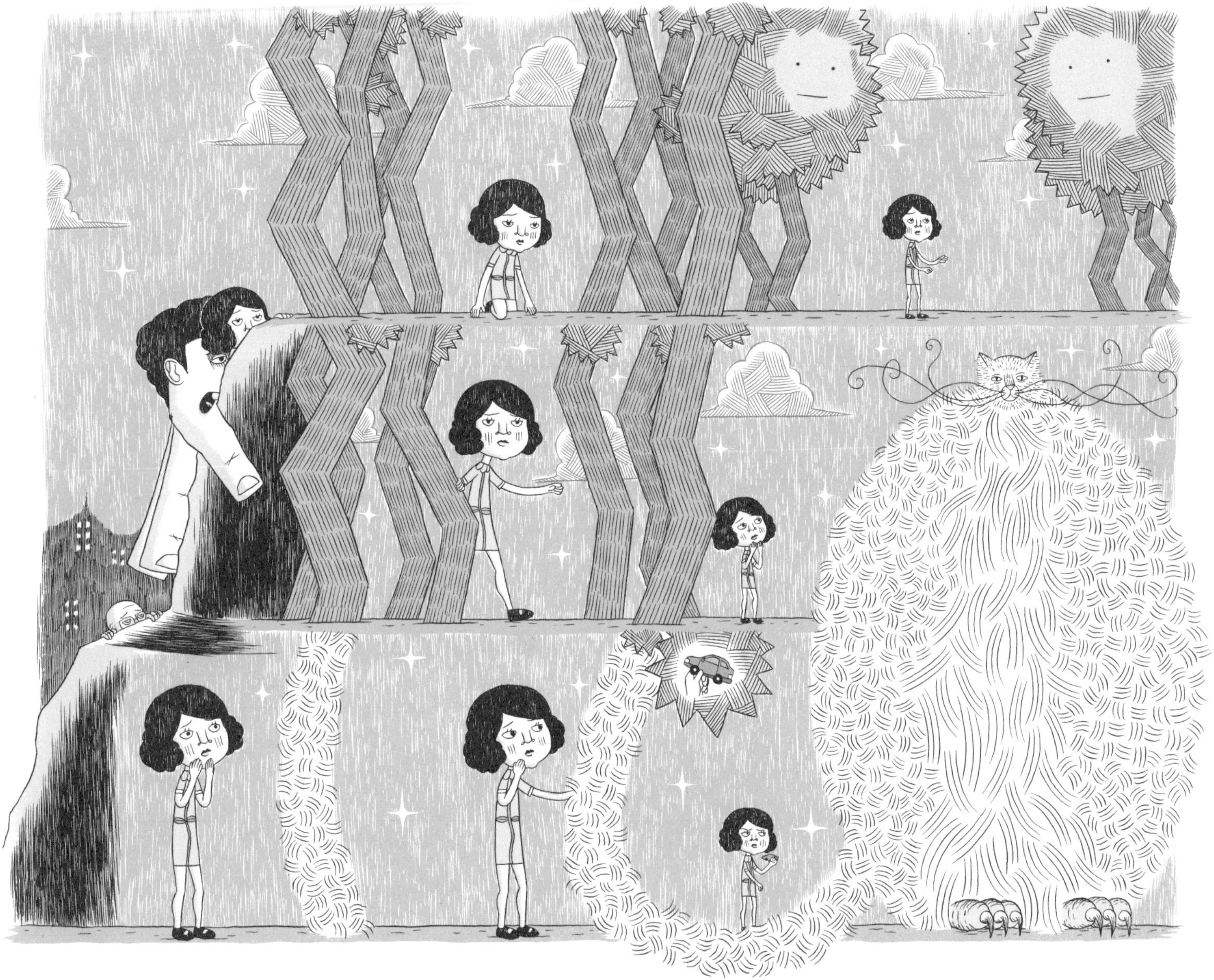

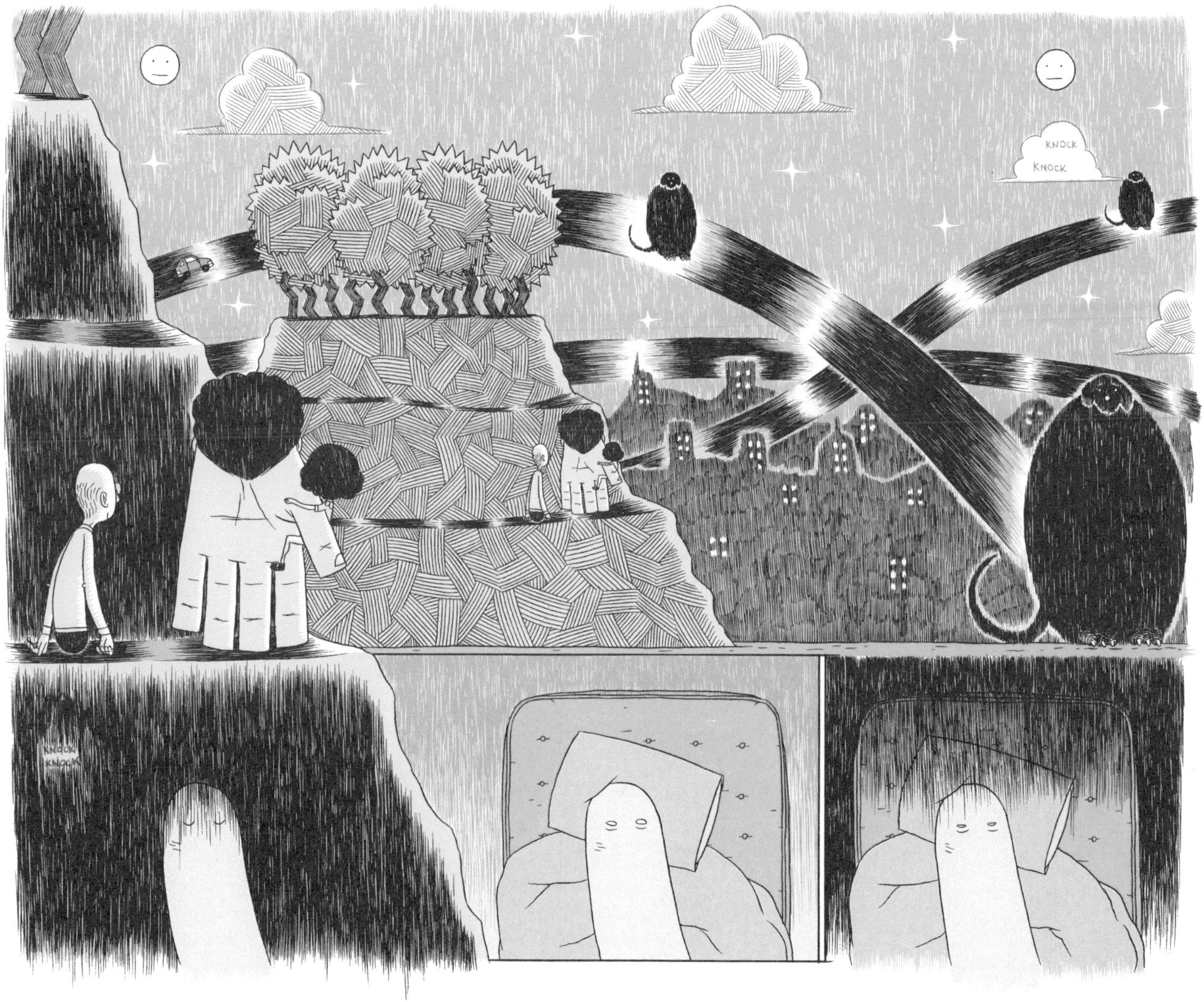
KNOCK
KNOCK
KNOCK
KNOCK

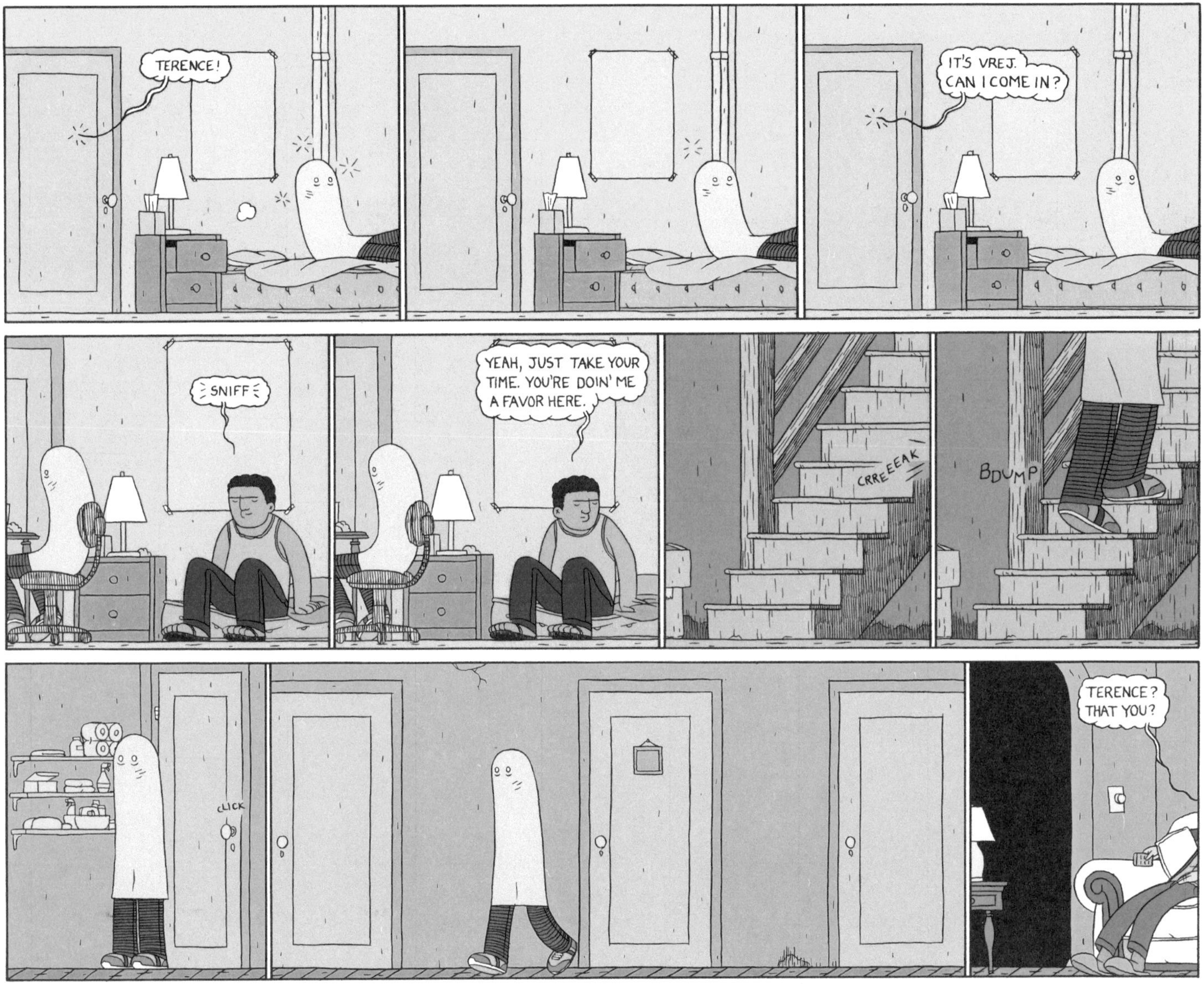
TERENCE!
IT'S VREJ. CAN I COME IN?
SNIFF
YEAH, JUST TAKE YOUR TIME. YOU'RE DOIN' ME A FAVOR HERE.
CRREEEAK
BDUMP
CLICK
TERENCE? THAT YOU?

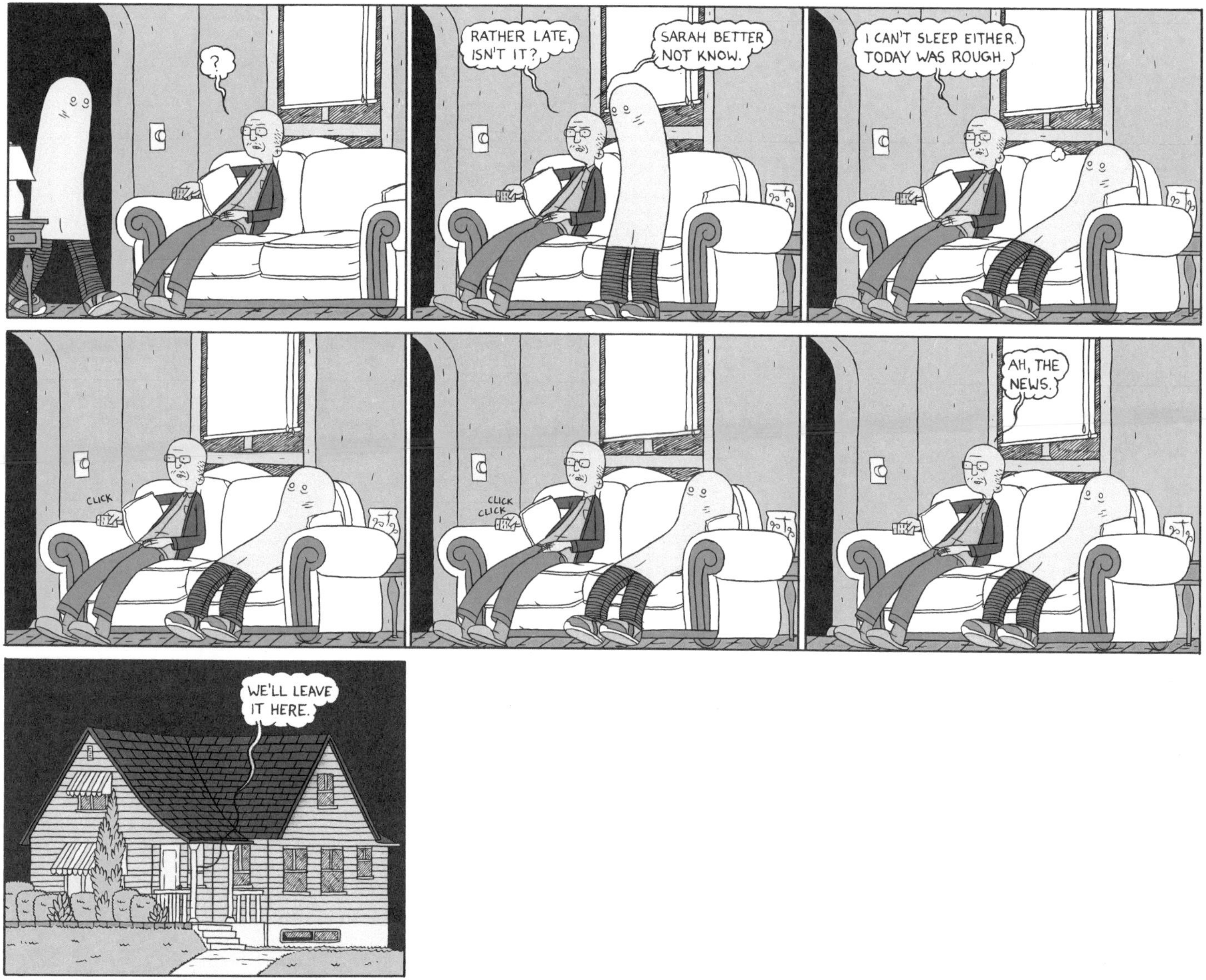
?
RATHER LATE, ISN'T IT?
SARAH BETTER NOT KNOW.
I CAN'T SLEEP EITHER. TODAY WAS ROUGH.
CLICK
CLICK CLICK
AH, THE NEWS.
WE'LL LEAVE IT HERE.

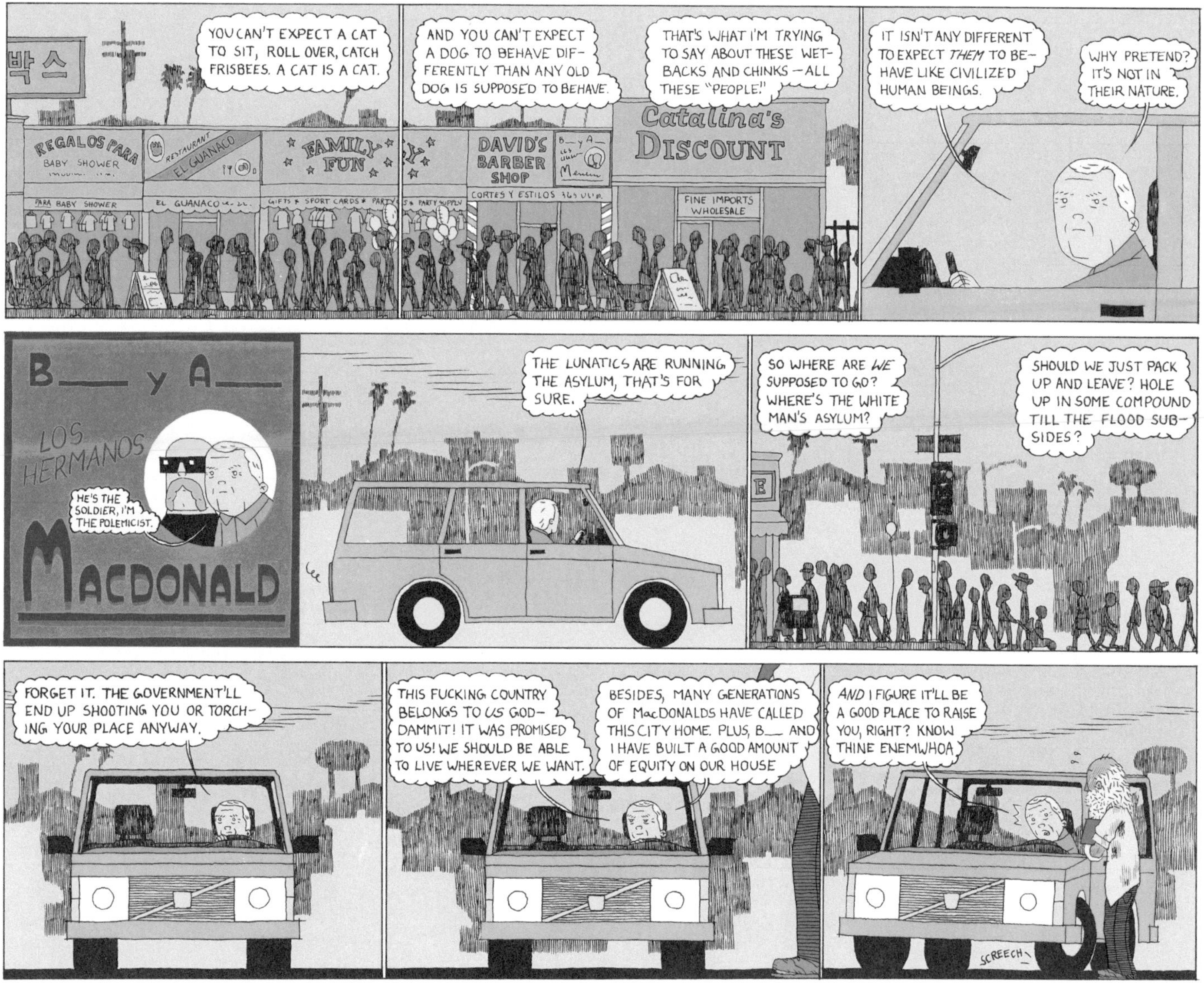
박스
REGALOS PARA BABY SHOWER
PARA BABY SHOWER
RESTAURANT EL GUANACO
EL GUANACO
FAMILY FUN
GIFTS * SPORT CARDS * PARTY
DAVID'S BARBER SHOP
CORTES Y ESTILOS
Catalina's DISCOUNT
FINE IMPORTS WHOLESALE
YOU CAN'T EXPECT A CAT TO SIT, ROLL OVER, CATCH FRISBEES. A CAT IS A CAT.
AND YOU CAN'T EXPECT A DOG TO BEHAVE DIFFERENTLY THAN ANY OLD DOG IS SUPPOSED TO BEHAVE.
THAT'S WHAT I'M TRYING TO SAY ABOUT THESE WETBACKS AND CHINKS — ALL THESE "PEOPLE."
IT ISN'T ANY DIFFERENT TO EXPECT THEM TO BEHAVE LIKE CIVILIZED HUMAN BEINGS.
WHY PRETEND? IT'S NOT IN THEIR NATURE.
B___ y A___
LOS HERMANOS
HE'S THE SOLDIER, I'M THE POLEMICIST.
MACDONALD
THE LUNATICS ARE RUNNING THE ASYLUM, THAT'S FOR SURE.
SO WHERE ARE WE SUPPOSED TO GO? WHERE'S THE WHITE MAN'S ASYLUM?
SHOULD WE JUST PACK UP AND LEAVE? HOLE UP IN SOME COMPOUND TILL THE FLOOD SUBSIDES?
FORGET IT. THE GOVERNMENT'LL END UP SHOOTING YOU OR TORCHING YOUR PLACE ANYWAY.
THIS FUCKING COUNTRY BELONGS TO US GODDAMMIT! IT WAS PROMISED TO US! WE SHOULD BE ABLE TO LIVE WHEREVER WE WANT.
BESIDES, MANY GENERATIONS OF MacDONALDS HAVE CALLED THIS CITY HOME. PLUS, B___ AND I HAVE BUILT A GOOD AMOUNT OF EQUITY ON OUR HOUSE
AND I FIGURE IT'LL BE A GOOD PLACE TO RAISE YOU, RIGHT? KNOW THINE ENEMWHOA
SCREECH

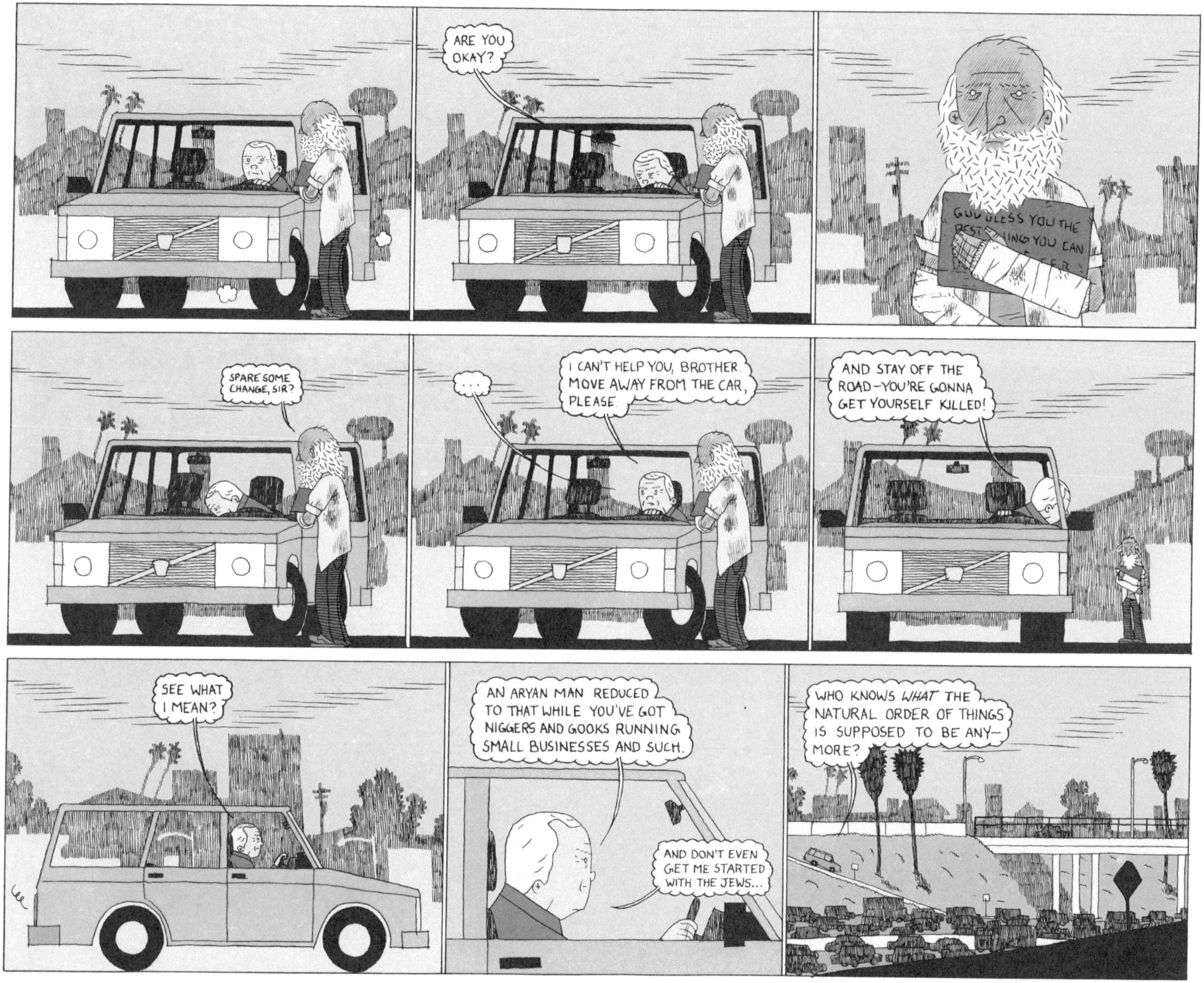
ARE YOU OKAY?
SPARE SOME CHANGE, SIR?
. . .
I CAN'T HELP YOU, BROTHER. MOVE AWAY FROM THE CAR, PLEASE.
AND STAY OFF THE ROAD–YOU'RE GONNA GET YOURSELF KILLED!
SEE WHAT I MEAN?
AN ARYAN MAN REDUCED TO THAT WHILE YOU'VE GOT NIGGERS AND GOOKS RUNNING SMALL BUSINESSES AND SUCH.
AND DON'T EVEN GET ME STARTED WITH THE JEWS...
WHO KNOWS *WHAT* THE NATURAL ORDER OF THINGS IS SUPPOSED TO BE ANY– MORE?

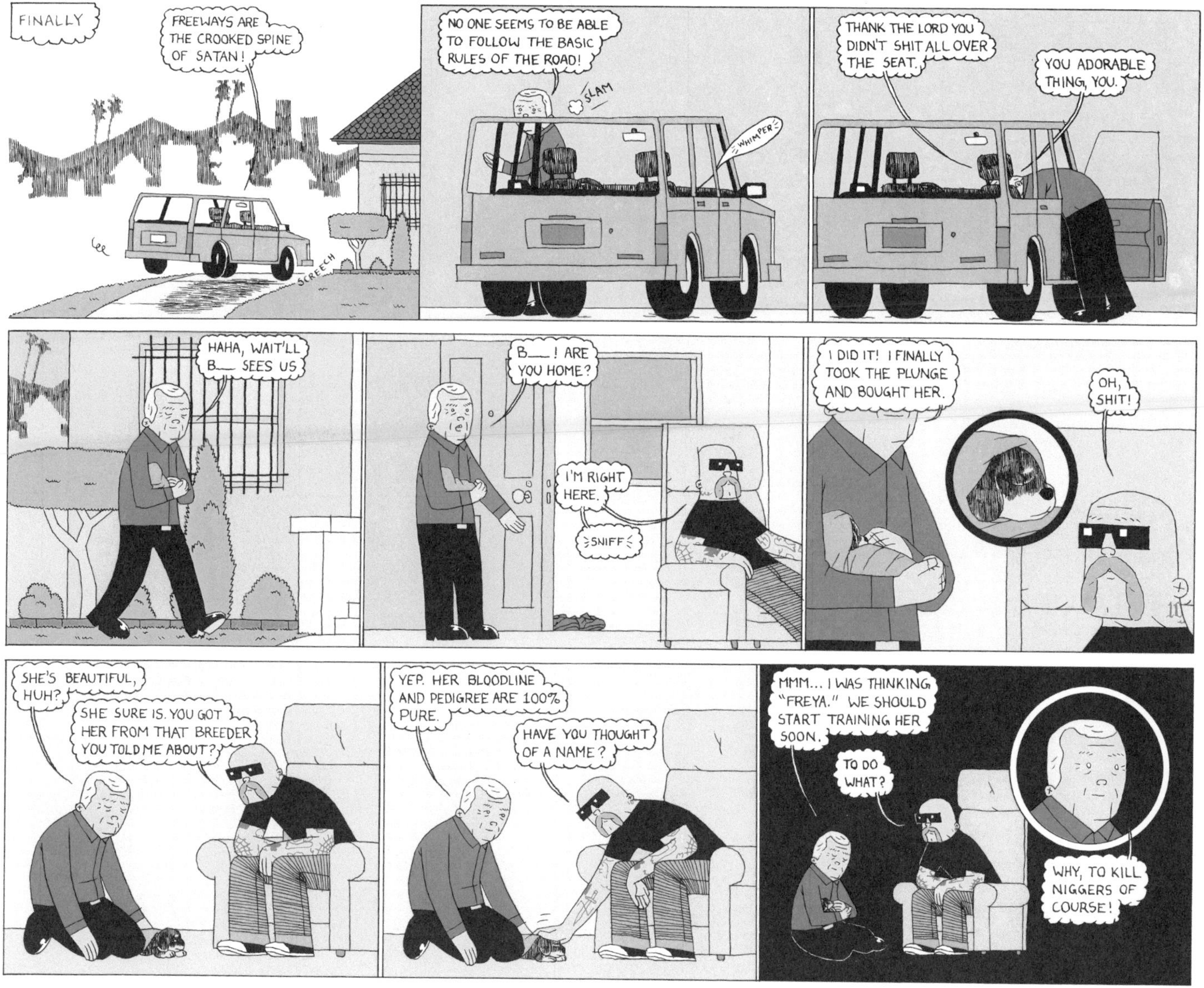
FINALLY
FREEWAYS ARE THE CROOKED SPINE OF SATAN!
SCREECH
NO ONE SEEMS TO BE ABLE TO FOLLOW THE BASIC RULES OF THE ROAD!
SLAM
WHIMPER
THANK THE LORD YOU DIDN'T SHIT ALL OVER THE SEAT.
YOU ADORABLE THING, YOU.
HAHA, WAIT'LL B___ SEES US.
B___! ARE YOU HOME?
I'M RIGHT HERE.
SNIFF
I DID IT! I FINALLY TOOK THE PLUNGE AND BOUGHT HER.
OH, SHIT!
SHE'S BEAUTIFUL, HUH?
SHE SURE IS. YOU GOT HER FROM THAT BREEDER YOU TOLD ME ABOUT?
YEP. HER BLOODLINE AND PEDIGREE ARE 100% PURE.
HAVE YOU THOUGHT OF A NAME?
MMM... I WAS THINKING "FREYA." WE SHOULD START TRAINING HER SOON.
TO DO WHAT?
WHY, TO KILL NIGGERS OF COURSE!

Meet Me

SNIFF

I guess empty's a sort of lifestyle for me

I'm here now, driving home, and I can't stop thinking about these weird dreams I keep having, I'm fumbling around for the used bag of C I know I dropped here somewhere and already my hands have that naughty sort of anticipatory tingle to them, kind of just this side of the nervous shakes, I might be drooling a little too

I'm there, by some ocean, standing at the edge of what I guess is a balcony (it's not always clear) or sometimes it's a cliff, and then I drop off

It's hot in the car, unbearably hot, I can't turn on the AC because I'm afraid it'd burn off whatever minute amount of gas I have left that much faster, my dreams usually involve me running away from something totally implacable and weird

I can't usually figure out what it is either, this thing that's chasing me, I have a feeling it has something to do with a crime I've committed in that dream world or whatever, there's a low, continuous noise droning outside my car right now that sounds like a very large washing machine

Something military? So right up there with the being-chased-by-something-implacable-dreams are the ones where I see my parents

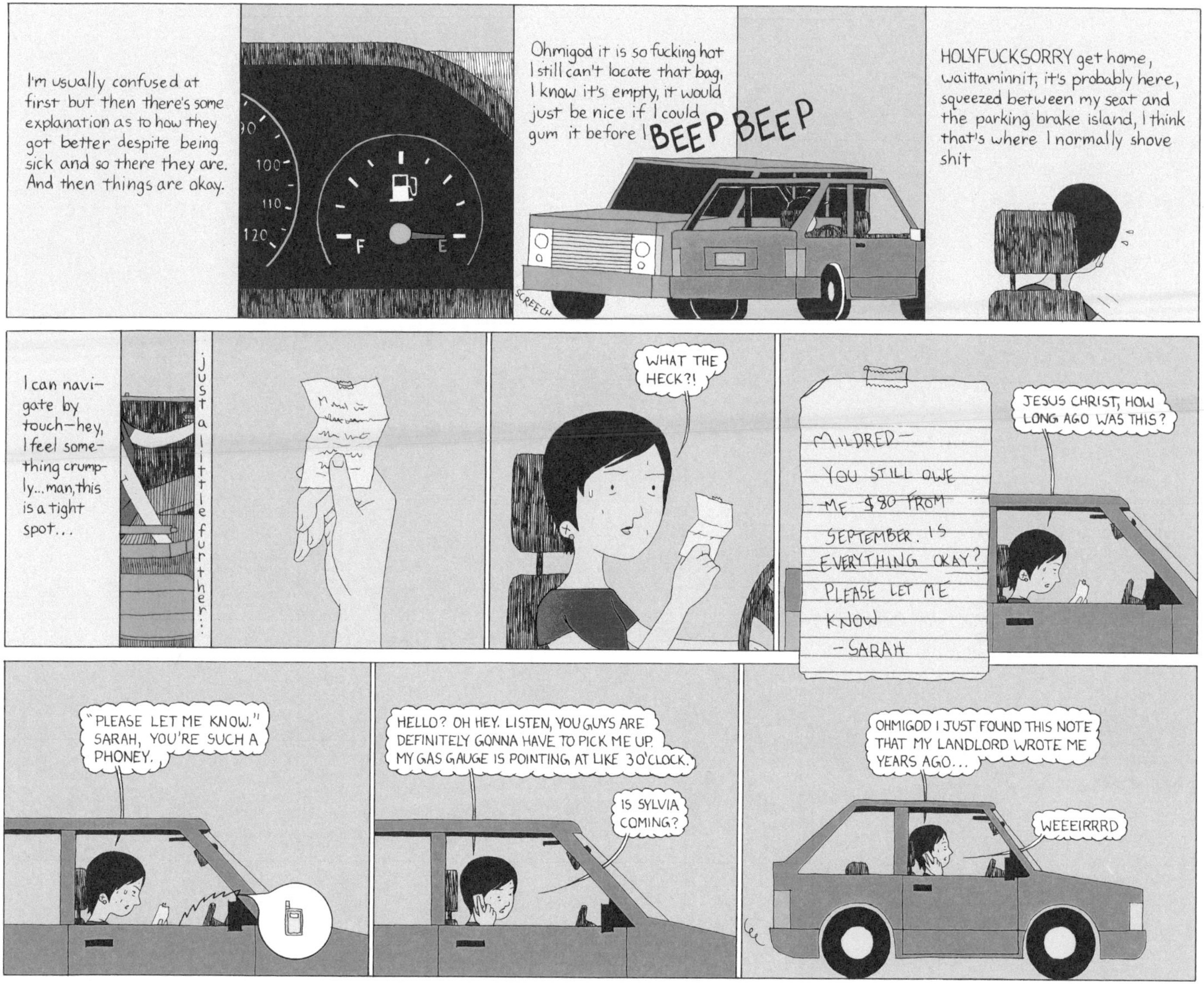

I'm usually confused at first but then there's some explanation as to how they got better despite being sick and so there they are. And then things are okay.
F
E
100
110
120
Ohmigod it is so fucking hot I still can't locate that bag, I know it's empty, it would just be nice if I could gum it before I
BEEP BEEP
SCREECH
HOLYFUCKSORRY get home, waittaminnit, it's probably here, squeezed between my seat and the parking brake island, I think that's where I normally shove shit
I can navigate by touch—hey, I feel something crumply...man, this is a tight spot...
just a little further...
WHAT THE HECK?!
MILDRED— YOU STILL OWE ME $80 FROM SEPTEMBER. IS EVERYTHING OKAY? PLEASE LET ME KNOW —SARAH
JESUS CHRIST, HOW LONG AGO WAS THIS?
"PLEASE LET ME KNOW." SARAH, YOU'RE SUCH A PHONEY.
HELLO? OH HEY. LISTEN, YOU GUYS ARE DEFINITELY GONNA HAVE TO PICK ME UP. MY GAS GAUGE IS POINTING AT LIKE 3 O'CLOCK.
IS SYLVIA COMING?
OHMIGOD I JUST FOUND THIS NOTE THAT MY LANDLORD WROTE ME YEARS AGO...
WEEEIRRRD

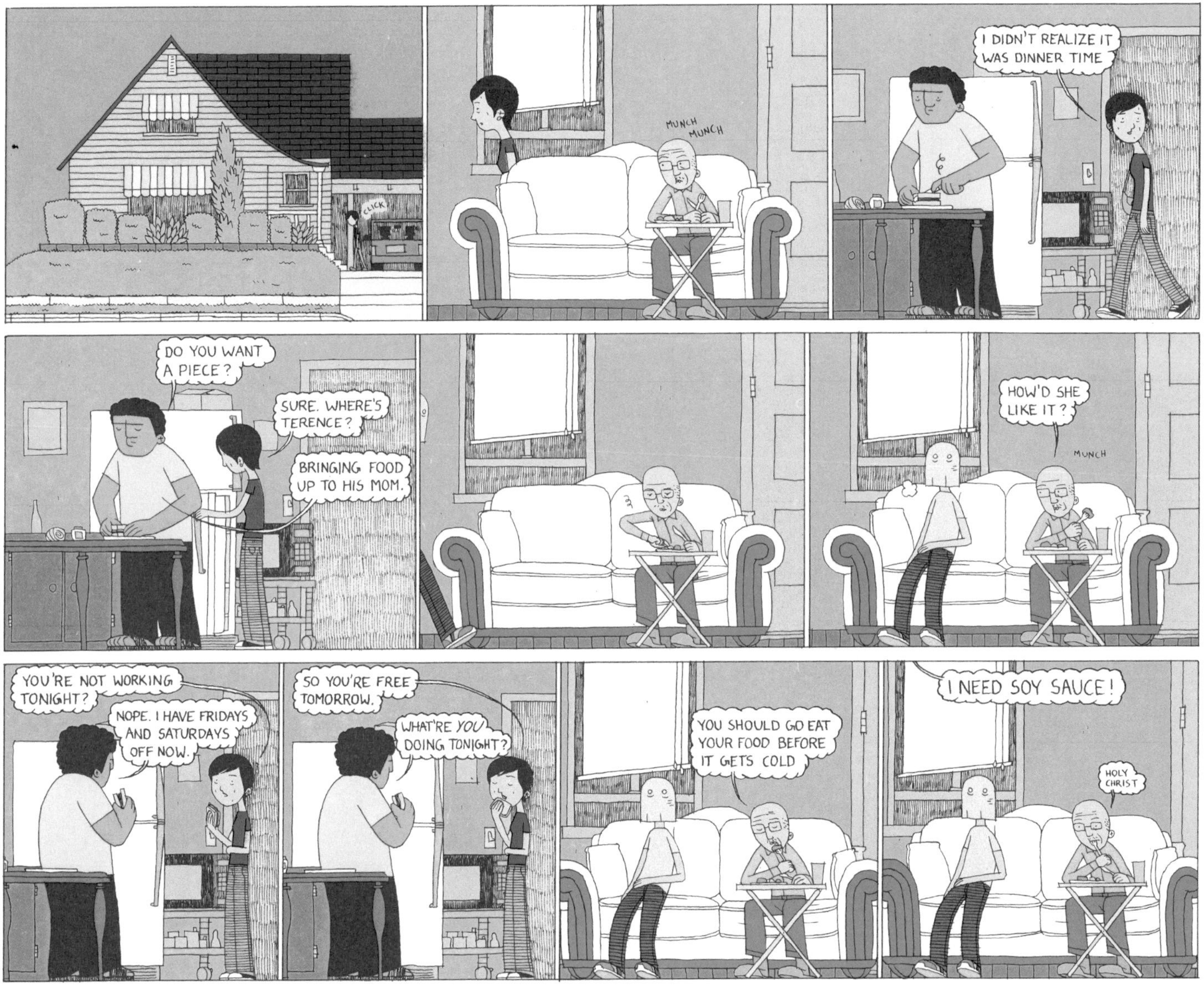
CLICK
MUNCH MUNCH
I DIDN'T REALIZE IT WAS DINNER TIME
DO YOU WANT A PIECE?
SURE. WHERE'S TERENCE?
BRINGING FOOD UP TO HIS MOM.
HOW'D SHE LIKE IT?
MUNCH
YOU'RE NOT WORKING TONIGHT?
NOPE. I HAVE FRIDAYS AND SATURDAYS OFF NOW.
SO YOU'RE FREE TOMORROW.
WHAT'RE *YOU* DOING TONIGHT?
YOU SHOULD GO EAT YOUR FOOD BEFORE IT GETS COLD
I NEED SOY SAUCE!
HOLY CHRIST

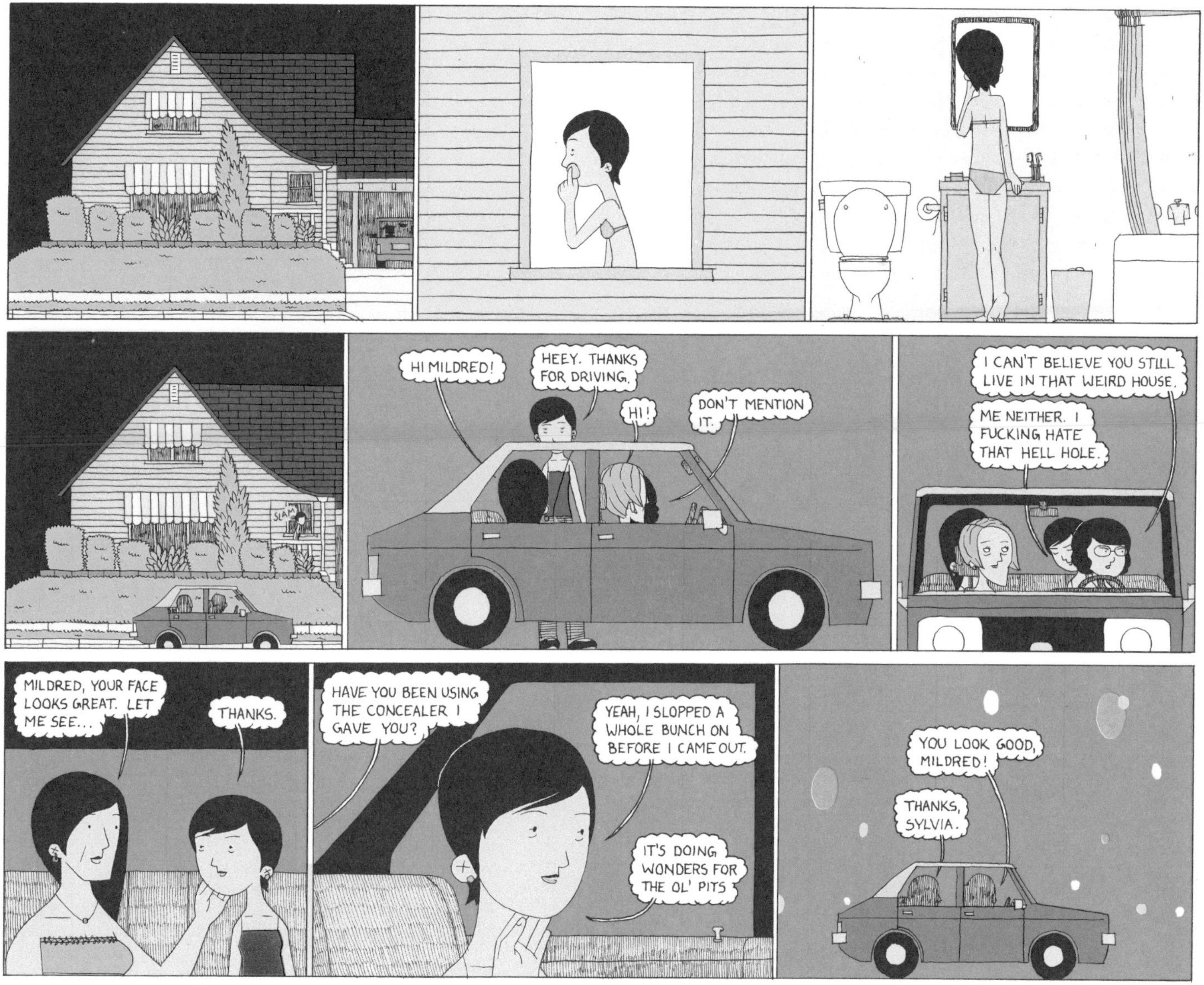
SLAM
HI MILDRED!
HEEY. THANKS FOR DRIVING.
HI!
DON'T MENTION IT.
I CAN'T BELIEVE YOU STILL LIVE IN THAT WEIRD HOUSE.
ME NEITHER. I FUCKING HATE THAT HELL HOLE.
MILDRED, YOUR FACE LOOKS GREAT. LET ME SEE...
THANKS.
HAVE YOU BEEN USING THE CONCEALER I GAVE YOU?
YEAH, I SLOPPED A WHOLE BUNCH ON BEFORE I CAME OUT.
IT'S DOING WONDERS FOR THE OL' PITS
YOU LOOK GOOD, MILDRED!
THANKS, SYLVIA.

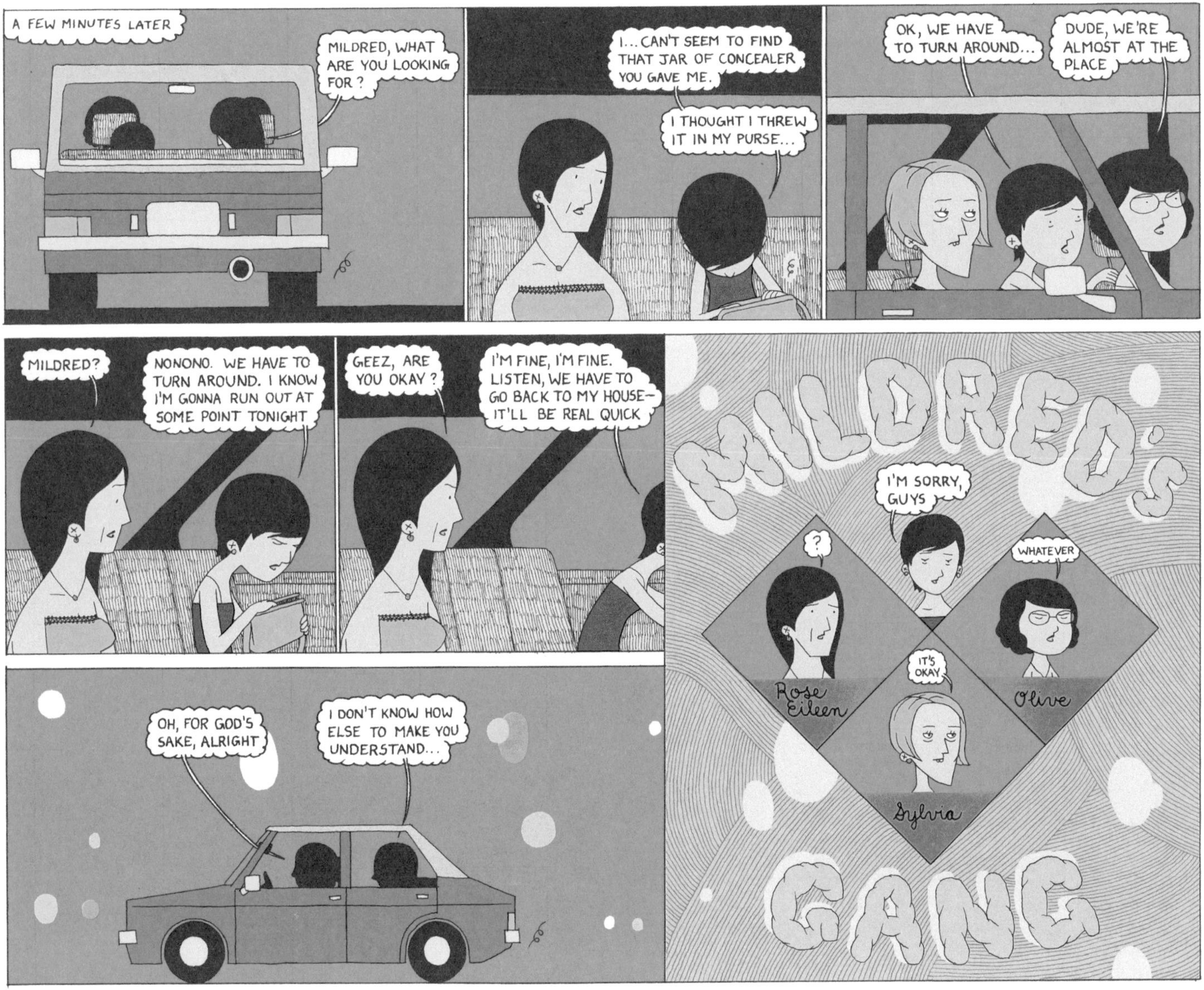
A FEW MINUTES LATER
MILDRED, WHAT ARE YOU LOOKING FOR ?
I... CAN'T SEEM TO FIND THAT JAR OF CONCEALER YOU GAVE ME.
I THOUGHT I THREW IT IN MY PURSE...
OK, WE HAVE TO TURN AROUND...
DUDE, WE'RE ALMOST AT THE PLACE
MILDRED?
NONONO. WE HAVE TO TURN AROUND. I KNOW I'M GONNA RUN OUT AT SOME POINT TONIGHT
GEEZ, ARE YOU OKAY ?
I'M FINE, I'M FINE. LISTEN, WE HAVE TO GO BACK TO MY HOUSE– IT'LL BE REAL QUICK
OH, FOR GOD'S SAKE, ALRIGHT
I DON'T KNOW HOW ELSE TO MAKE YOU UNDERSTAND...
MILDRED'S
I'M SORRY, GUYS
?
WHATEVER
IT'S OKAY
Rose Eileen
Olive
Sylvia
GANG

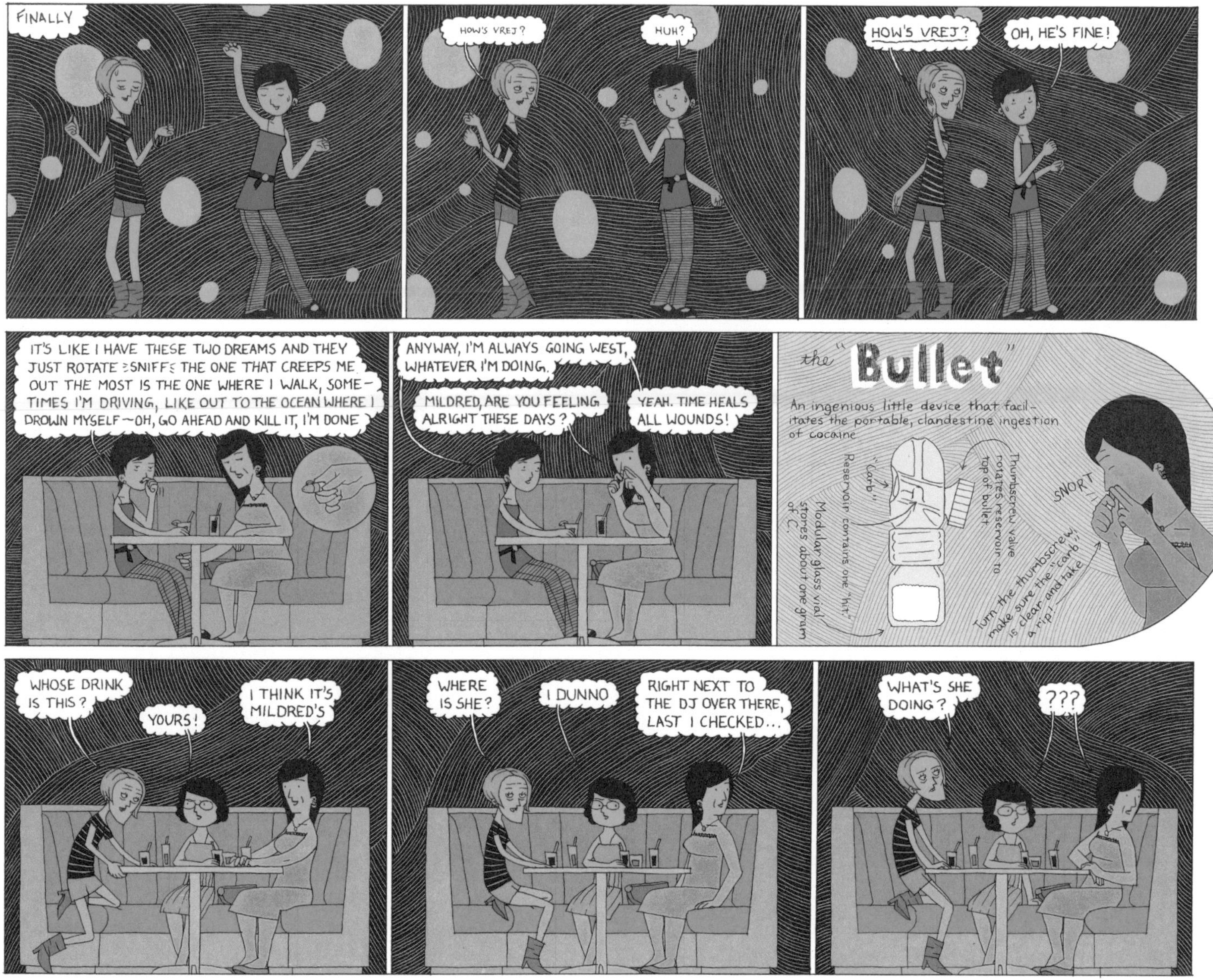
FINALLY
HOW'S VREJ?
HUH?
HOW'S VREJ?
OH, HE'S FINE!
IT'S LIKE I HAVE THESE TWO DREAMS AND THEY JUST ROTATE ≷SNIFF≷ THE ONE THAT CREEPS ME OUT THE MOST IS THE ONE WHERE I WALK, SOMETIMES I'M DRIVING, LIKE OUT TO THE OCEAN WHERE I DROWN MYSELF—OH, GO AHEAD AND KILL IT, I'M DONE
ANYWAY, I'M ALWAYS GOING WEST, WHATEVER I'M DOING.
MILDRED, ARE YOU FEELING ALRIGHT THESE DAYS?
YEAH. TIME HEALS ALL WOUNDS!
the "Bullet"
An ingenious little device that facilitates the portable, clandestine ingestion of cocaine
"Carb"
Reservoir contains one "hit."
Modular glass vial stores about one gram of C.
Thumbscrew valve rotates reservoir to top of bullet
SNORT
Turn the thumbscrew; make sure the "carb" is clear and take a rip!
WHOSE DRINK IS THIS?
YOURS!
I THINK IT'S MILDRED'S
WHERE IS SHE?
I DUNNO
RIGHT NEXT TO THE DJ OVER THERE, LAST I CHECKED...
WHAT'S SHE DOING?
???

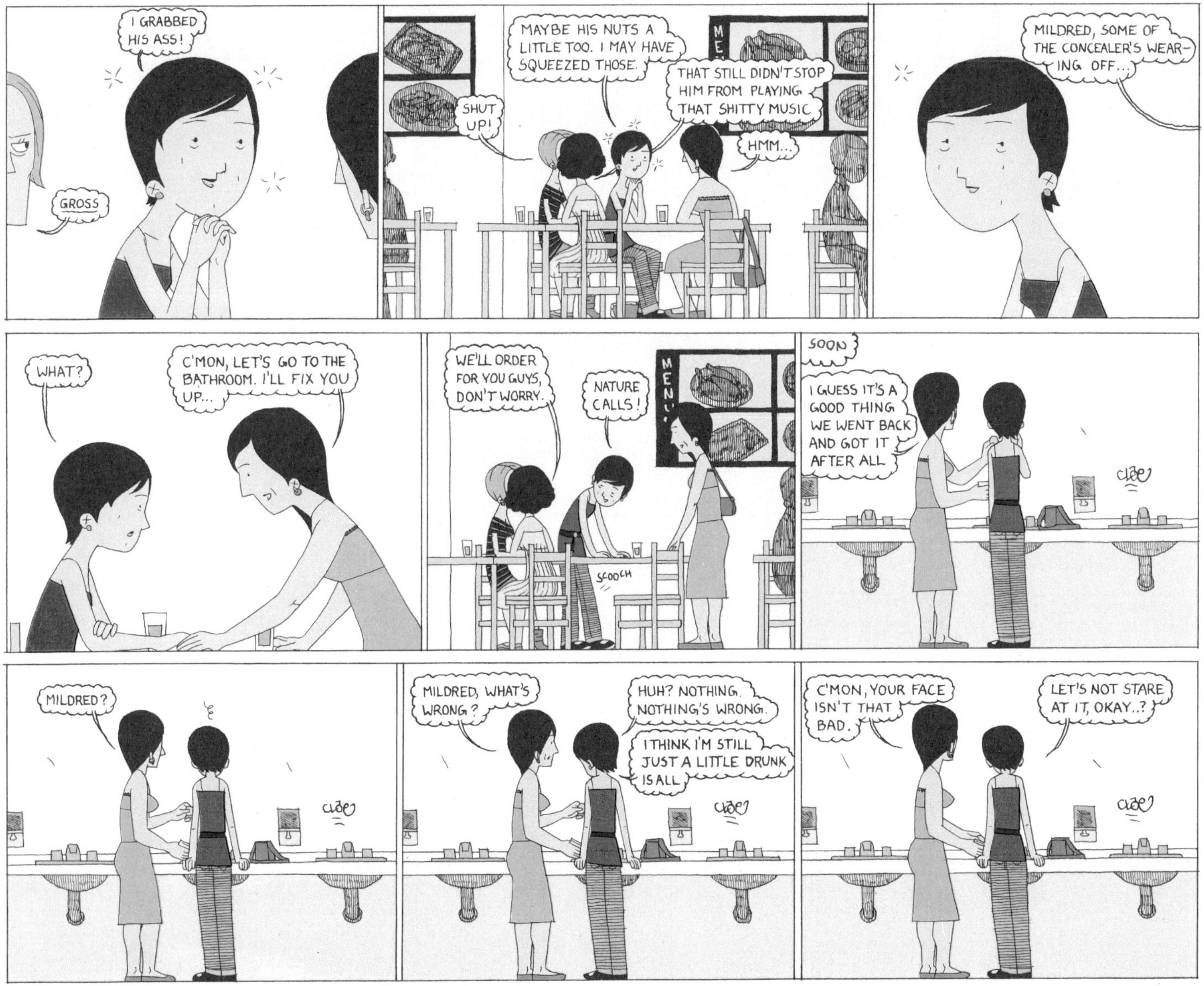
I GRABBED HIS ASS!
GROSS
SHUT UP!
MAYBE HIS NUTS A LITTLE TOO. I MAY HAVE SQUEEZED THOSE.
THAT STILL DIDN'T STOP HIM FROM PLAYING THAT SHITTY MUSIC.
HMM...
MILDRED, SOME OF THE CONCEALER'S WEARING OFF...
WHAT?
C'MON, LET'S GO TO THE BATHROOM. I'LL FIX YOU UP...
WE'LL ORDER FOR YOU GUYS, DON'T WORRY.
NATURE CALLS!
SCOOCH
SOON
I GUESS IT'S A GOOD THING WE WENT BACK AND GOT IT AFTER ALL
MILDRED?
MILDRED, WHAT'S WRONG?
HUH? NOTHING. NOTHING'S WRONG.
I THINK I'M STILL JUST A LITTLE DRUNK IS ALL
C'MON, YOUR FACE ISN'T THAT BAD.
LET'S NOT STARE AT IT, OKAY..?

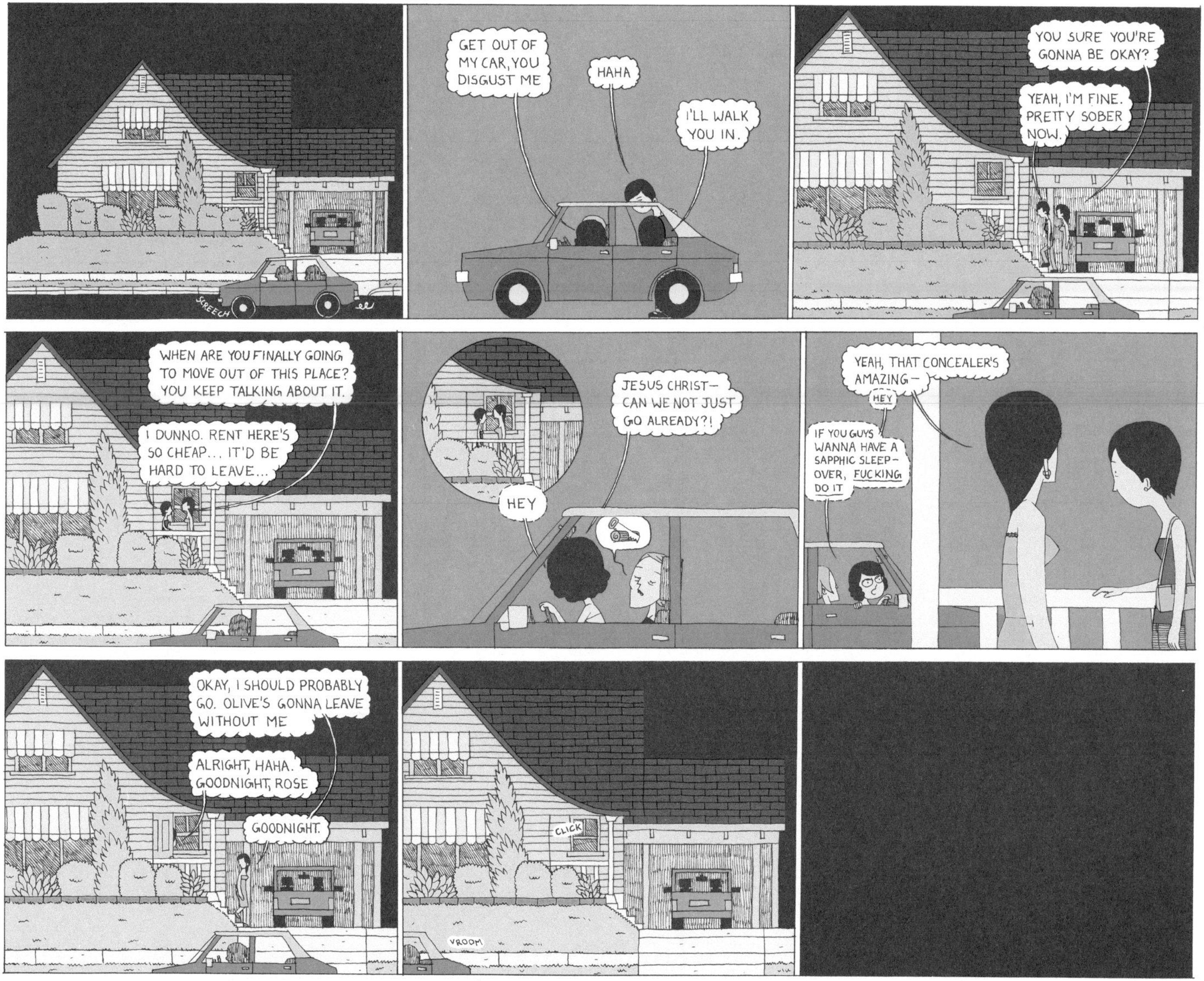
SCREECH
GET OUT OF MY CAR, YOU DISGUST ME
HAHA
I'LL WALK YOU IN.
YOU SURE YOU'RE GONNA BE OKAY?
YEAH, I'M FINE. PRETTY SOBER NOW.
WHEN ARE YOU FINALLY GOING TO MOVE OUT OF THIS PLACE? YOU KEEP TALKING ABOUT IT.
I DUNNO. RENT HERE'S SO CHEAP... IT'D BE HARD TO LEAVE...
HEY
JESUS CHRIST— CAN WE NOT JUST GO ALREADY?!
YEAH, THAT CONCEALER'S AMAZING—
HEY
IF YOU GUYS WANNA HAVE A SAPPHIC SLEEP-OVER, FUCKING DO IT
OKAY, I SHOULD PROBABLY GO. OLIVE'S GONNA LEAVE WITHOUT ME
ALRIGHT, HAHA. GOODNIGHT, ROSE
GOODNIGHT.
CLICK
VROOM

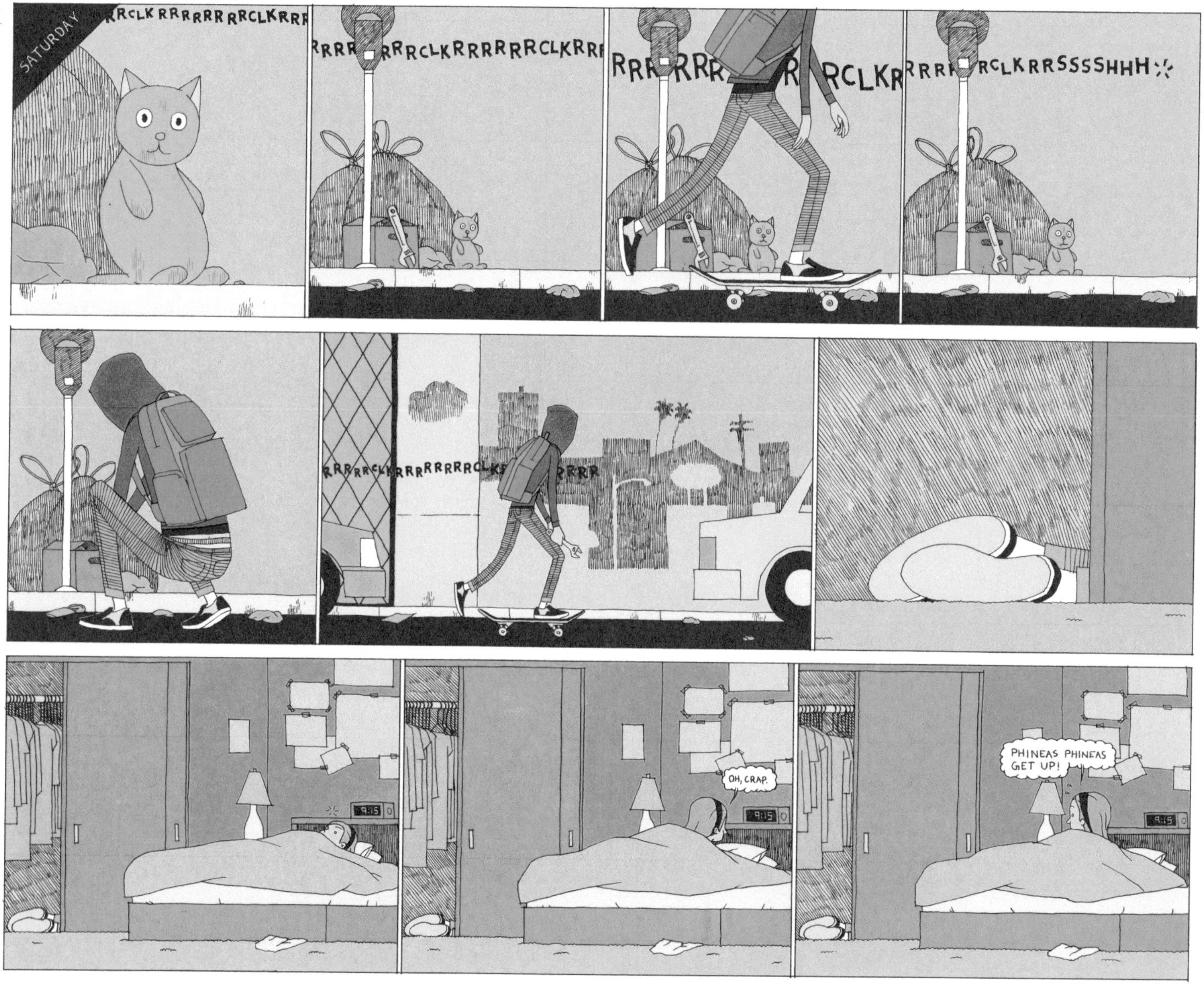
SATURDAY
RRCLK RRRRRRR RRCLKRRR
RRRR RRRCLKRRRRRRCLKRRR
RRR RRR R RCLKR
RRRR RCLKRRSSSSHHH
RRRRRRCLKRRRRRRRRRCLK RRRR
OH, CRAP.
PHINEAS PHINEAS GET UP!

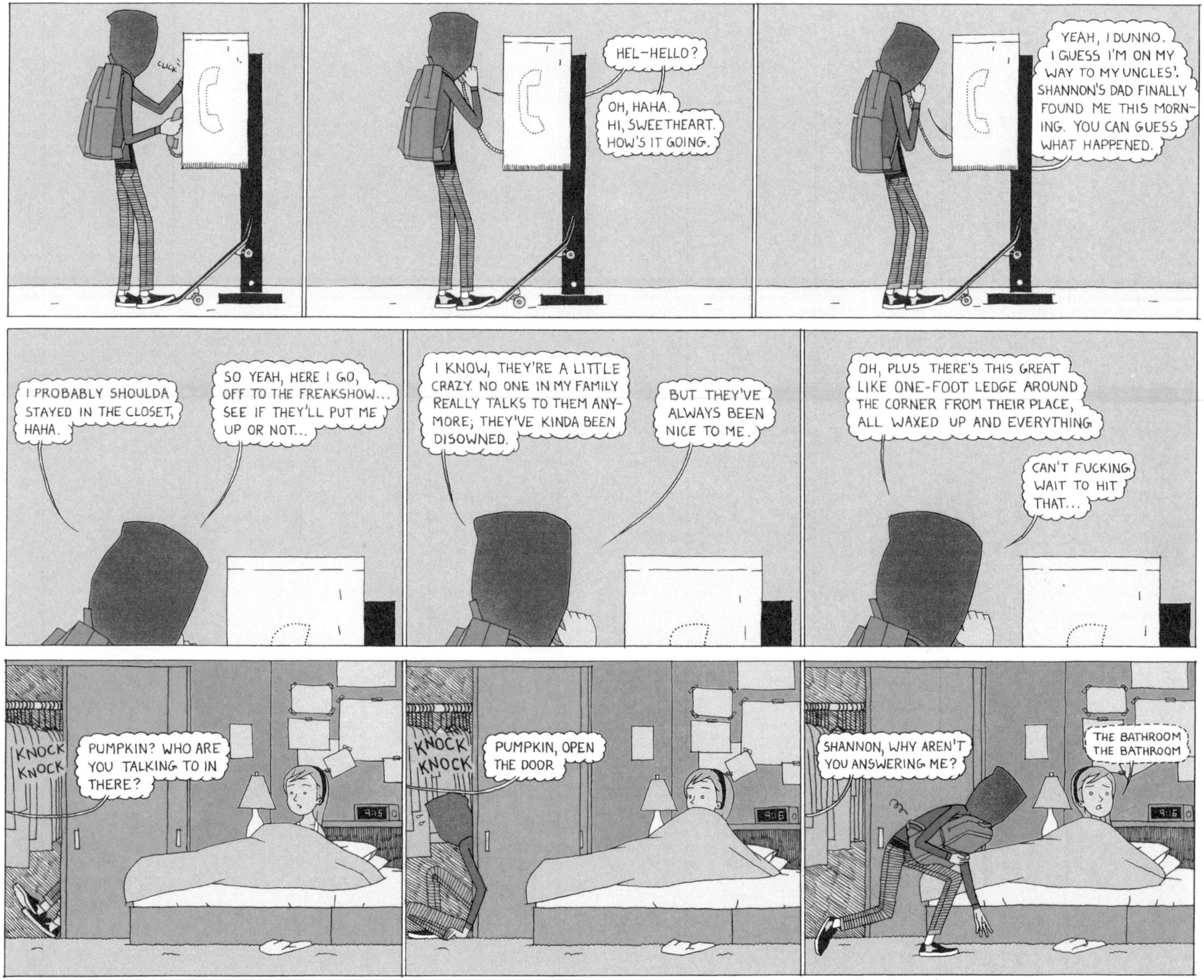
CLICK
HEL-HELLO?
OH, HAHA. HI, SWEETHEART. HOW'S IT GOING.
YEAH, I DUNNO. I GUESS I'M ON MY WAY TO MY UNCLES'. SHANNON'S DAD FINALLY FOUND ME THIS MORNING. YOU CAN GUESS WHAT HAPPENED.
I PROBABLY SHOULDA STAYED IN THE CLOSET, HAHA.
SO YEAH, HERE I GO, OFF TO THE FREAKSHOW... SEE IF THEY'LL PUT ME UP OR NOT...
I KNOW, THEY'RE A LITTLE CRAZY. NO ONE IN MY FAMILY REALLY TALKS TO THEM ANYMORE; THEY'VE KINDA BEEN DISOWNED.
BUT THEY'VE ALWAYS BEEN NICE TO ME.
OH, PLUS THERE'S THIS GREAT LIKE ONE-FOOT LEDGE AROUND THE CORNER FROM THEIR PLACE, ALL WAXED UP AND EVERYTHING.
CAN'T FUCKING WAIT TO HIT THAT...
KNOCK KNOCK
PUMPKIN? WHO ARE YOU TALKING TO IN THERE?
KNOCK KNOCK
PUMPKIN, OPEN THE DOOR
SHANNON, WHY AREN'T YOU ANSWERING ME?
THE BATHROOM THE BATHROOM

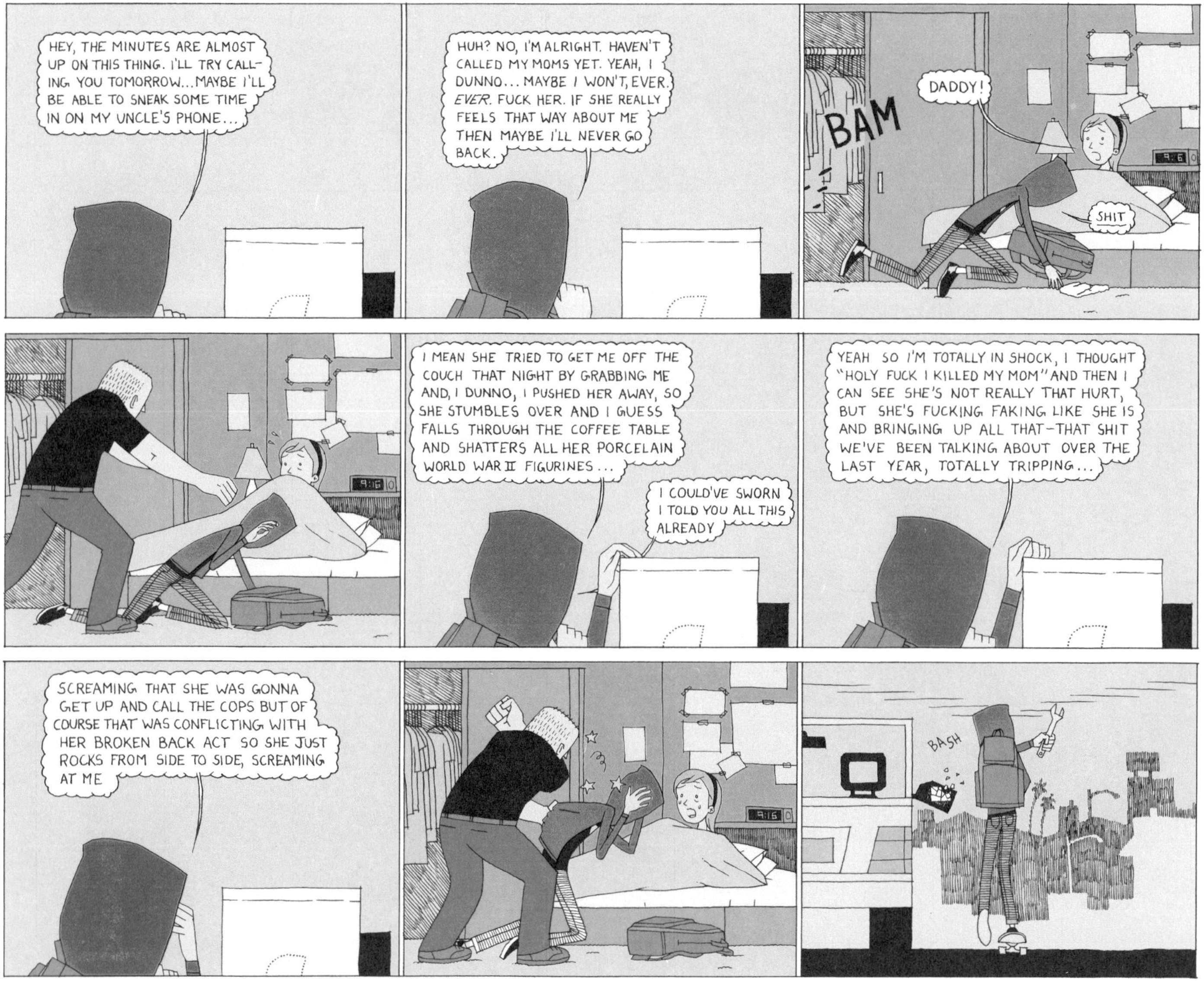

HEY, THE MINUTES ARE ALMOST UP ON THIS THING. I'LL TRY CALLING YOU TOMORROW... MAYBE I'LL BE ABLE TO SNEAK SOME TIME IN ON MY UNCLE'S PHONE...
HUH? NO, I'M ALRIGHT. HAVEN'T CALLED MY MOMS YET. YEAH, I DUNNO... MAYBE I WON'T, EVER. EVER. FUCK HER. IF SHE REALLY FEELS THAT WAY ABOUT ME THEN MAYBE I'LL NEVER GO BACK.
BAM
DADDY!
SHIT
I MEAN SHE TRIED TO GET ME OFF THE COUCH THAT NIGHT BY GRABBING ME AND, I DUNNO, I PUSHED HER AWAY, SO SHE STUMBLES OVER AND I GUESS FALLS THROUGH THE COFFEE TABLE AND SHATTERS ALL HER PORCELAIN WORLD WAR II FIGURINES...
I COULD'VE SWORN I TOLD YOU ALL THIS ALREADY
YEAH SO I'M TOTALLY IN SHOCK, I THOUGHT "HOLY FUCK I KILLED MY MOM" AND THEN I CAN SEE SHE'S NOT REALLY THAT HURT, BUT SHE'S FUCKING FAKING LIKE SHE IS AND BRINGING UP ALL THAT—THAT SHIT WE'VE BEEN TALKING ABOUT OVER THE LAST YEAR, TOTALLY TRIPPING...
SCREAMING THAT SHE WAS GONNA GET UP AND CALL THE COPS BUT OF COURSE THAT WAS CONFLICTING WITH HER BROKEN BACK ACT SO SHE JUST ROCKS FROM SIDE TO SIDE, SCREAMING AT ME
BASH

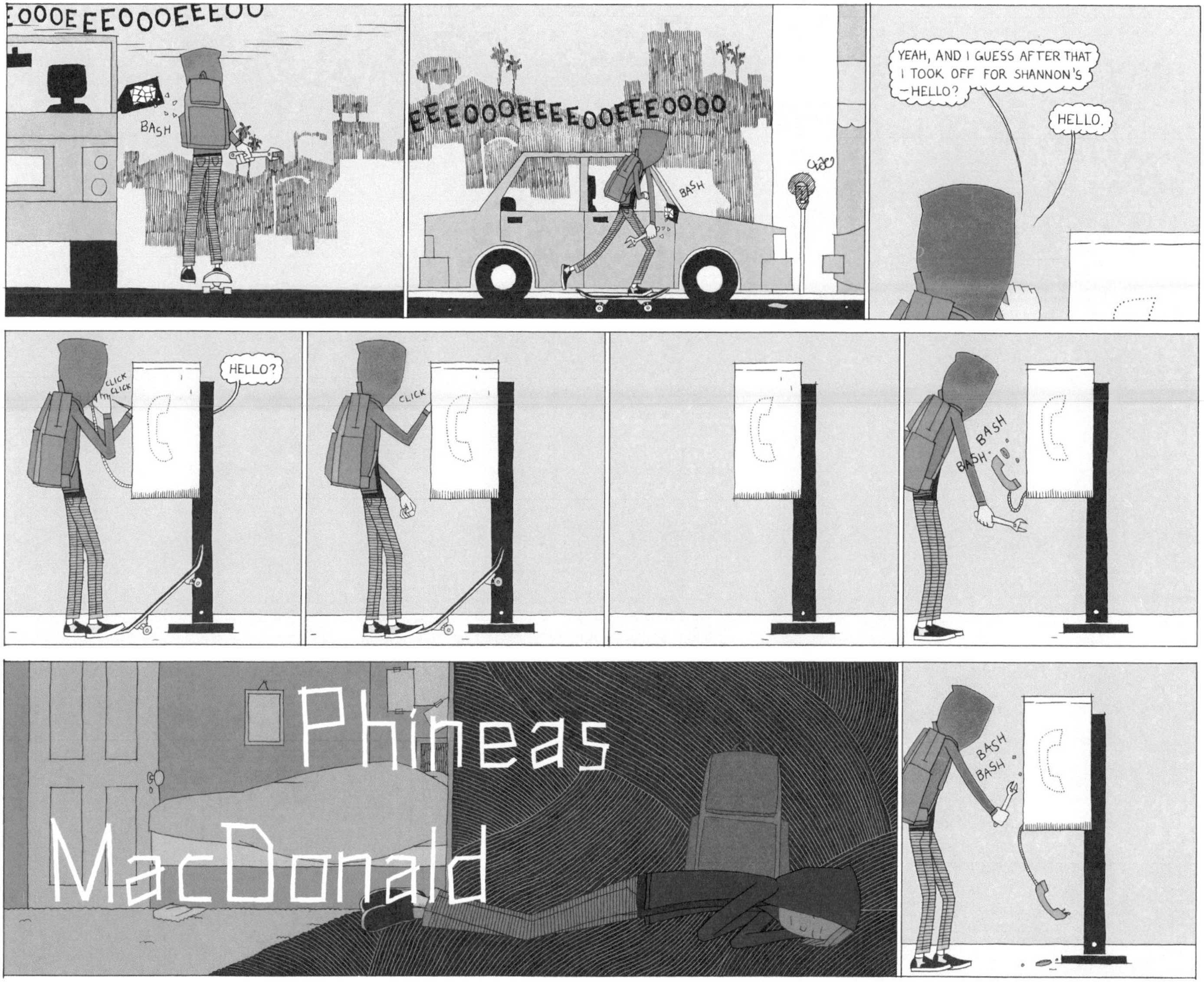

EOOOEEEOOOEEEOO
BASH
EEEOOOEEEEOOEEEOOOO
BASH
YEAH, AND I GUESS AFTER THAT I TOOK OFF FOR SHANNON'S —HELLO?
HELLO.
CLICK CLICK
HELLO?
CLICK
BASH
BASH
Phineas MacDonald
BASH
BASH

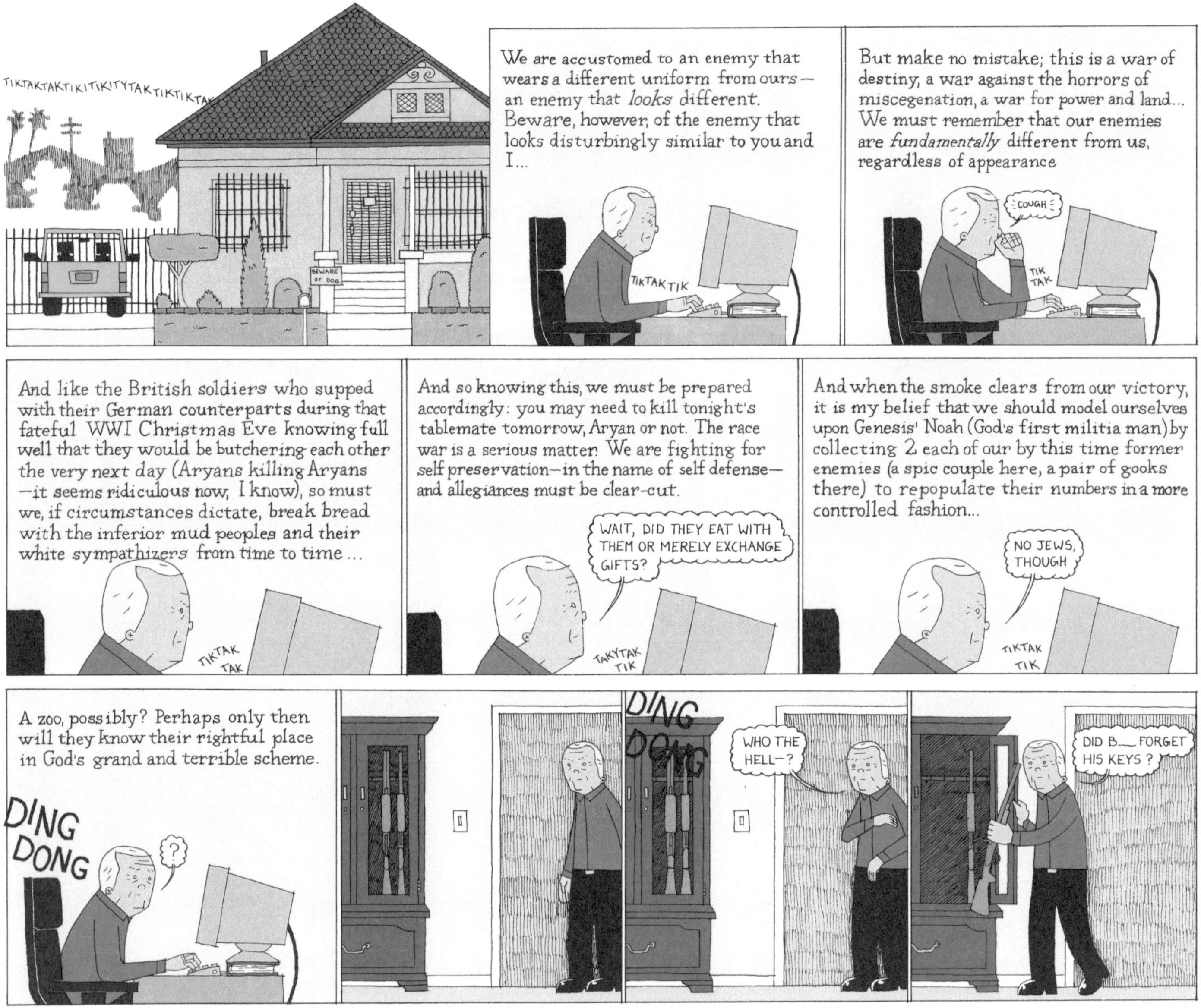
TIKTAKTAKTIKITIKITYTAKTIKTIKTAK
BEWARE OF DOG
We are accustomed to an enemy that wears a different uniform from ours—an enemy that *looks* different. Beware, however, of the enemy that looks disturbingly similar to you and I...
TIKTAKTIK
But make no mistake; this is a war of destiny, a war against the horrors of miscegenation, a war for power and land... We must remember that our enemies are *fundamentally* different from us, regardless of appearance
COUGH
TIK TAK
And like the British soldiers who supped with their German counterparts during that fateful WWI Christmas Eve knowing full well that they would be butchering each other the very next day (Aryans killing Aryans—it seems ridiculous now, I know), so must we, if circumstances dictate, break bread with the inferior mud peoples and their white sympathizers from time to time...
TIKTAK TAK
And so knowing this, we must be prepared accordingly: you may need to kill tonight's tablemate tomorrow, Aryan or not. The race war is a serious matter. We are fighting for self preservation—in the name of self defense—and allegiances must be clear-cut.
WAIT, DID THEY EAT WITH THEM OR MERELY EXCHANGE GIFTS?
TAKYTAK TIK
And when the smoke clears from our victory, it is my belief that we should model ourselves upon Genesis' Noah (God's first militia man) by collecting 2 each of our by this time former enemies (a spic couple here, a pair of gooks there) to repopulate their numbers in a more controlled fashion...
NO JEWS, THOUGH
TIKTAK TIK
A zoo, possibly? Perhaps only then will they know their rightful place in God's grand and terrible scheme.
DING DONG
?
DING DONG
WHO THE HELL—?
DID B___ FORGET HIS KEYS?

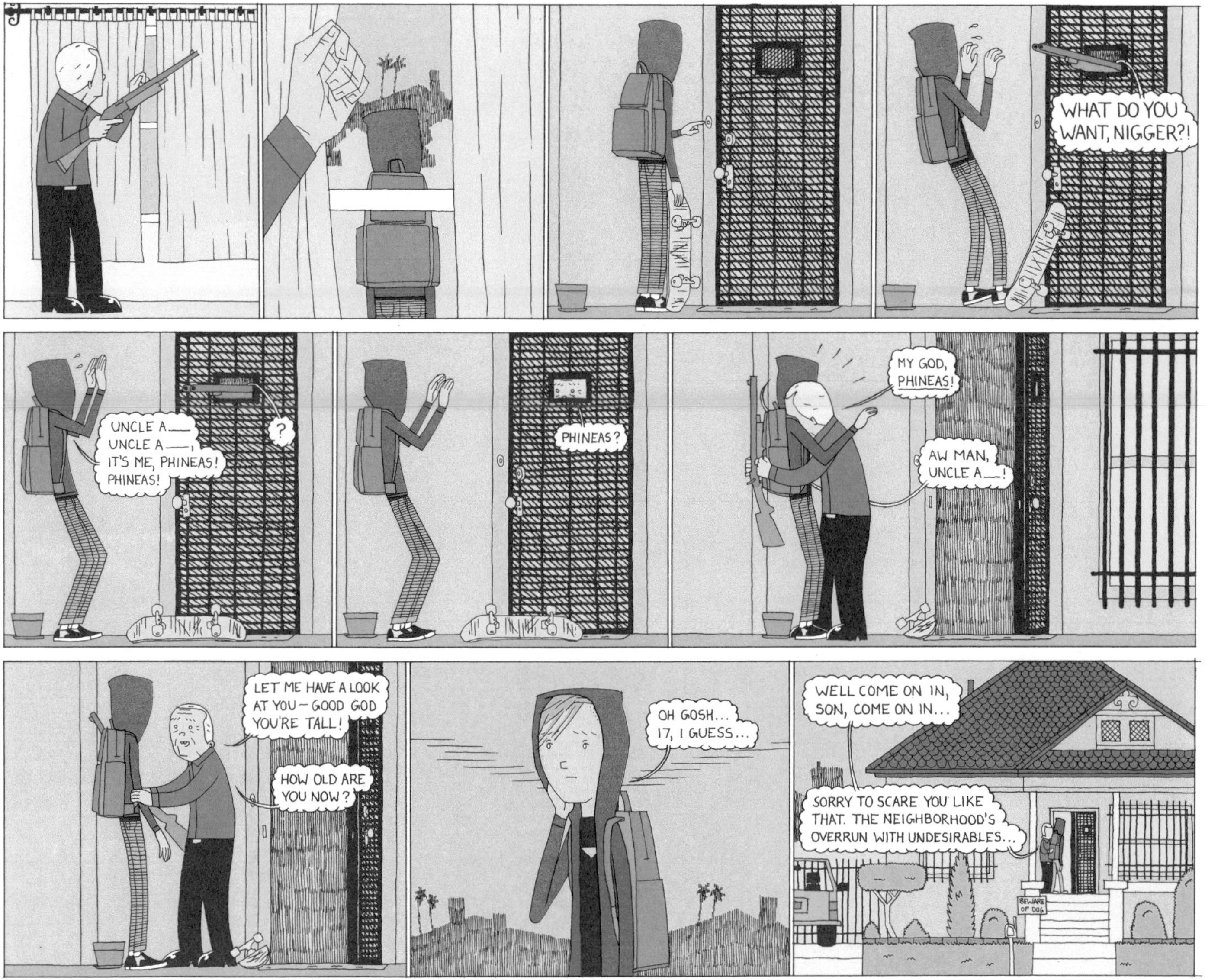
WHAT DO YOU WANT, NIGGER?!
UNCLE A___ UNCLE A___, IT'S ME, PHINEAS! PHINEAS!
?
PHINEAS?
MY GOD, PHINEAS!
AW MAN, UNCLE A___!
LET ME HAVE A LOOK AT YOU—GOOD GOD YOU'RE TALL!
HOW OLD ARE YOU NOW?
OH GOSH... 17, I GUESS...
WELL COME ON IN, SON, COME ON IN...
SORRY TO SCARE YOU LIKE THAT. THE NEIGHBORHOOD'S OVERRUN WITH UNDESIRABLES...
BEWARE OF DOG

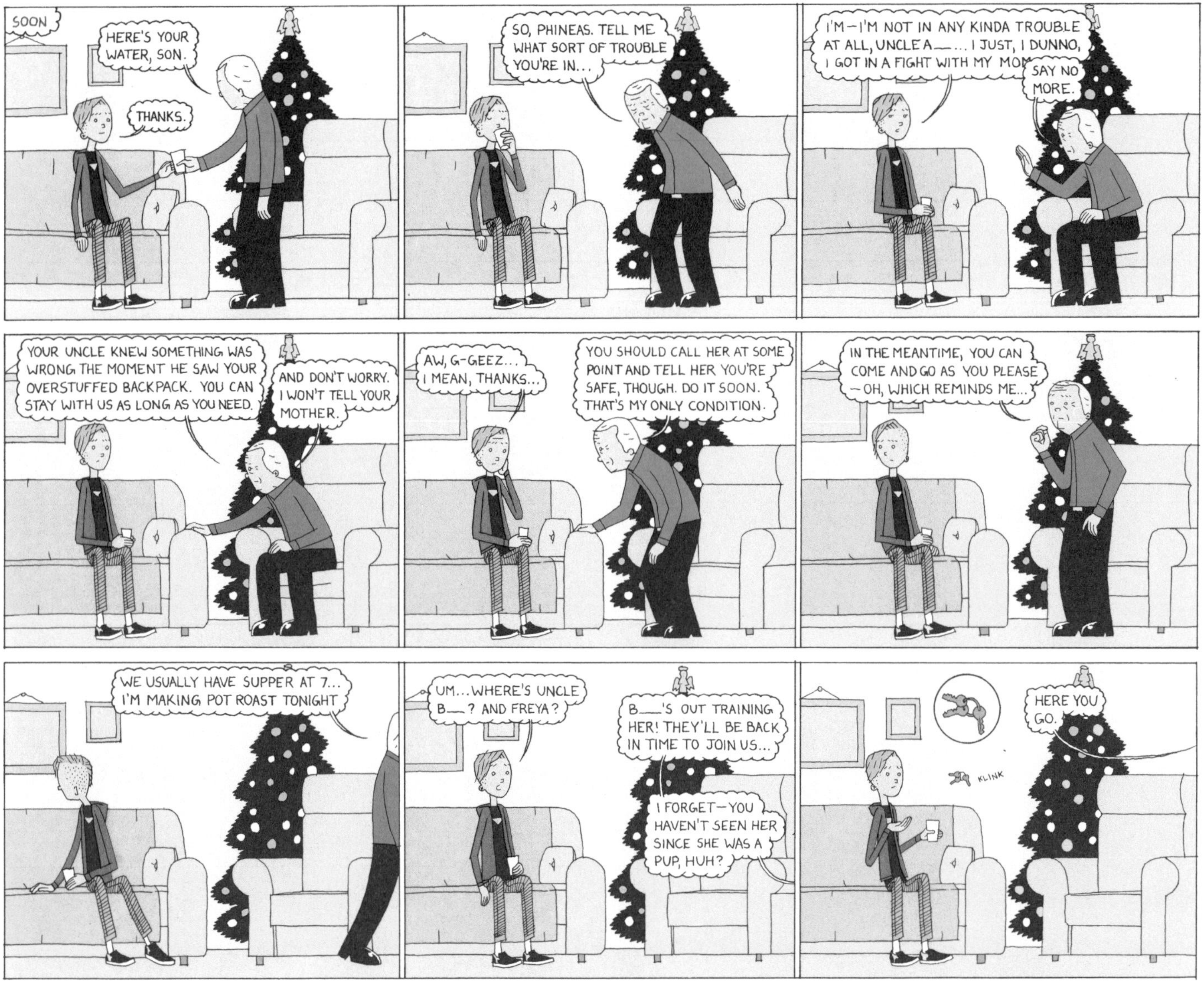
SOON
HERE'S YOUR WATER, SON.
THANKS.
SO, PHINEAS. TELL ME WHAT SORT OF TROUBLE YOU'RE IN...
I'M—I'M NOT IN ANY KINDA TROUBLE AT ALL, UNCLE A___... I JUST, I DUNNO, I GOT IN A FIGHT WITH MY MOM
SAY NO MORE.
YOUR UNCLE KNEW SOMETHING WAS WRONG THE MOMENT HE SAW YOUR OVERSTUFFED BACKPACK. YOU CAN STAY WITH US AS LONG AS YOU NEED.
AND DON'T WORRY. I WON'T TELL YOUR MOTHER.
AW, G-GEEZ... I MEAN, THANKS...
YOU SHOULD CALL HER AT SOME POINT AND TELL HER YOU'RE SAFE, THOUGH. DO IT SOON. THAT'S MY ONLY CONDITION.
IN THE MEANTIME, YOU CAN COME AND GO AS YOU PLEASE —OH, WHICH REMINDS ME...
WE USUALLY HAVE SUPPER AT 7... I'M MAKING POT ROAST TONIGHT
UM... WHERE'S UNCLE B___? AND FREYA?
B___'S OUT TRAINING HER! THEY'LL BE BACK IN TIME TO JOIN US...
I FORGET—YOU HAVEN'T SEEN HER SINCE SHE WAS A PUP, HUH?
HERE YOU GO.
KLINK

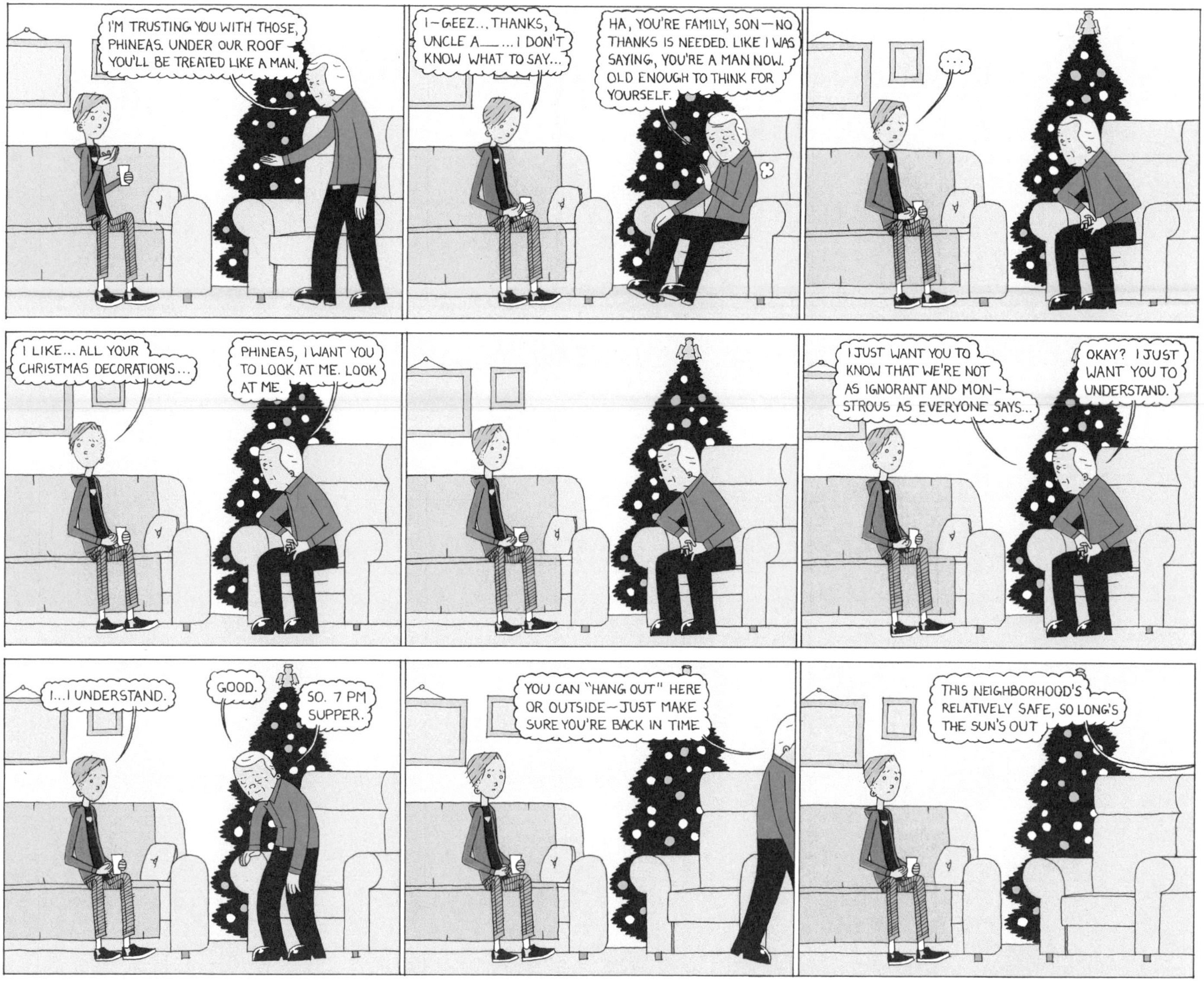
I'M TRUSTING YOU WITH THOSE, PHINEAS. UNDER OUR ROOF YOU'LL BE TREATED LIKE A MAN.
I—GEEZ..., THANKS, UNCLE A___... I DON'T KNOW WHAT TO SAY...
HA, YOU'RE FAMILY, SON—NO THANKS IS NEEDED. LIKE I WAS SAYING, YOU'RE A MAN NOW. OLD ENOUGH TO THINK FOR YOURSELF.
...
I LIKE... ALL YOUR CHRISTMAS DECORATIONS...
PHINEAS, I WANT YOU TO LOOK AT ME. LOOK AT ME.
I JUST WANT YOU TO KNOW THAT WE'RE NOT AS IGNORANT AND MON-STROUS AS EVERYONE SAYS...
OKAY? I JUST WANT YOU TO UNDERSTAND.
I... I UNDERSTAND.
GOOD.
SO. 7 PM SUPPER.
YOU CAN "HANG OUT" HERE OR OUTSIDE—JUST MAKE SURE YOU'RE BACK IN TIME.
THIS NEIGHBORHOOD'S RELATIVELY SAFE, SO LONG'S THE SUN'S OUT

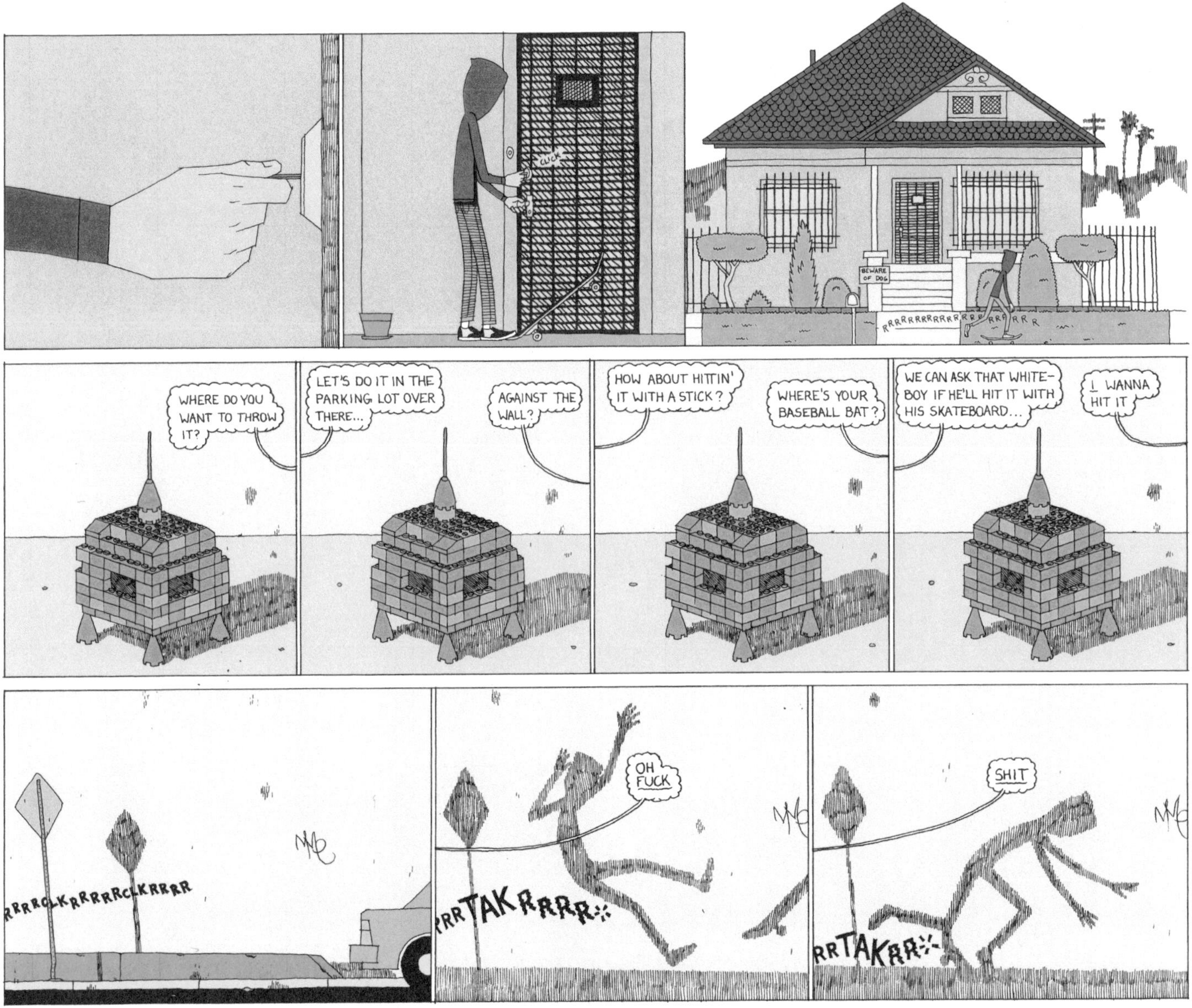
CLICK
BEWARE OF DOG
RRRRRRRRRRRRRRRRRRRRR
WHERE DO YOU WANT TO THROW IT?
LET'S DO IT IN THE PARKING LOT OVER THERE...
AGAINST THE WALL?
HOW ABOUT HITTIN' IT WITH A STICK?
WHERE'S YOUR BASEBALL BAT?
WE CAN ASK THAT WHITE-BOY IF HE'LL HIT IT WITH HIS SKATEBOARD...
I WANNA HIT IT
RRRRCLKRRRRRCLKRRRR
OH FUCK
RRRTAKRRRR
SHIT
RRTAKRR

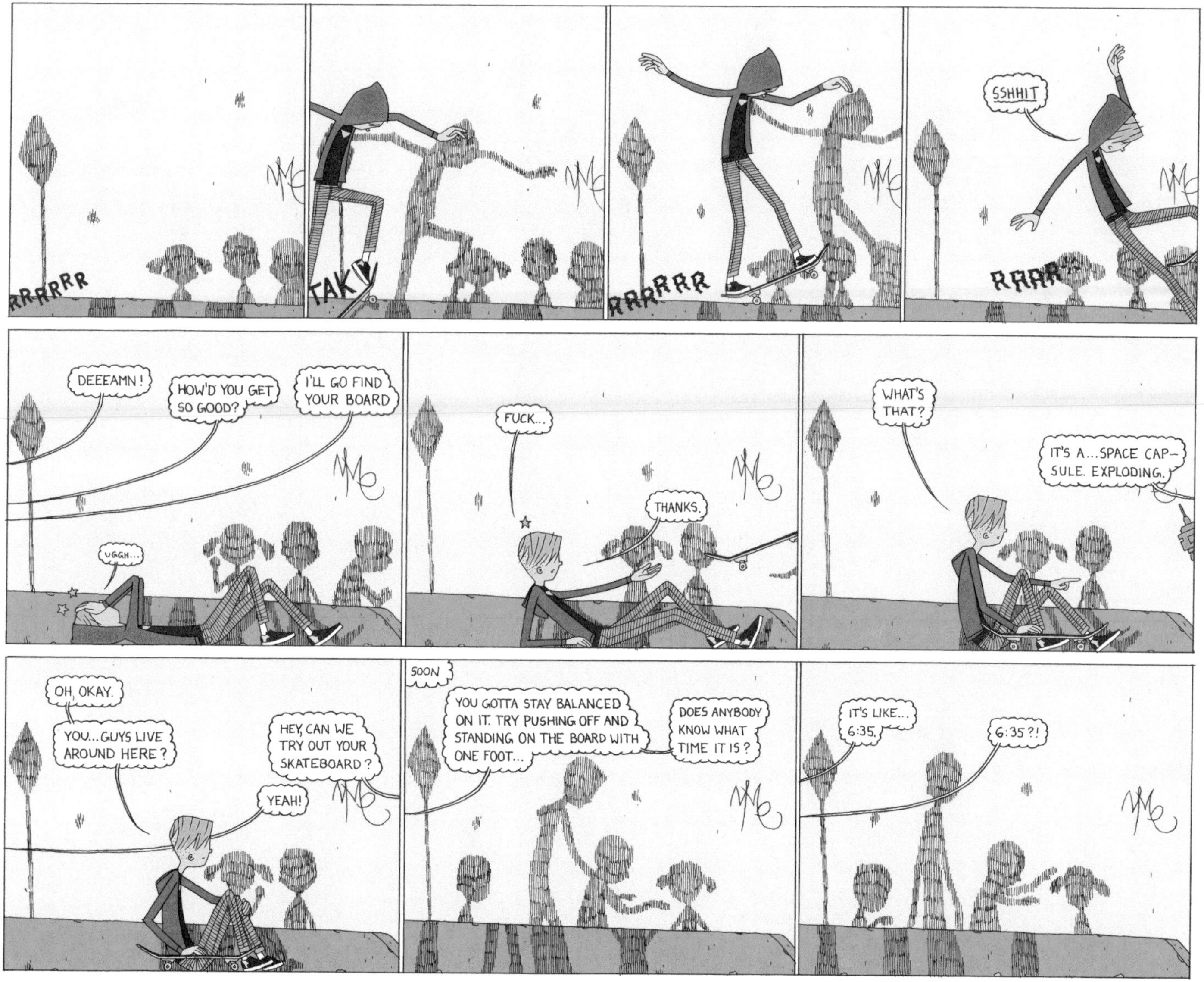
RRRRRRR
TAK
RRRRRRR
SSHHIT
RRRR
DEEEAMN!
HOW'D YOU GET SO GOOD?
I'LL GO FIND YOUR BOARD
UGGH...
FUCK...
THANKS.
WHAT'S THAT?
IT'S A...SPACE CAP-SULE. EXPLODING.
OH, OKAY.
YOU...GUYS LIVE AROUND HERE?
HEY, CAN WE TRY OUT YOUR SKATEBOARD?
YEAH!
SOON
YOU GOTTA STAY BALANCED ON IT. TRY PUSHING OFF AND STANDING ON THE BOARD WITH ONE FOOT...
DOES ANYBODY KNOW WHAT TIME IT IS?
IT'S LIKE... 6:35,
6:35?!

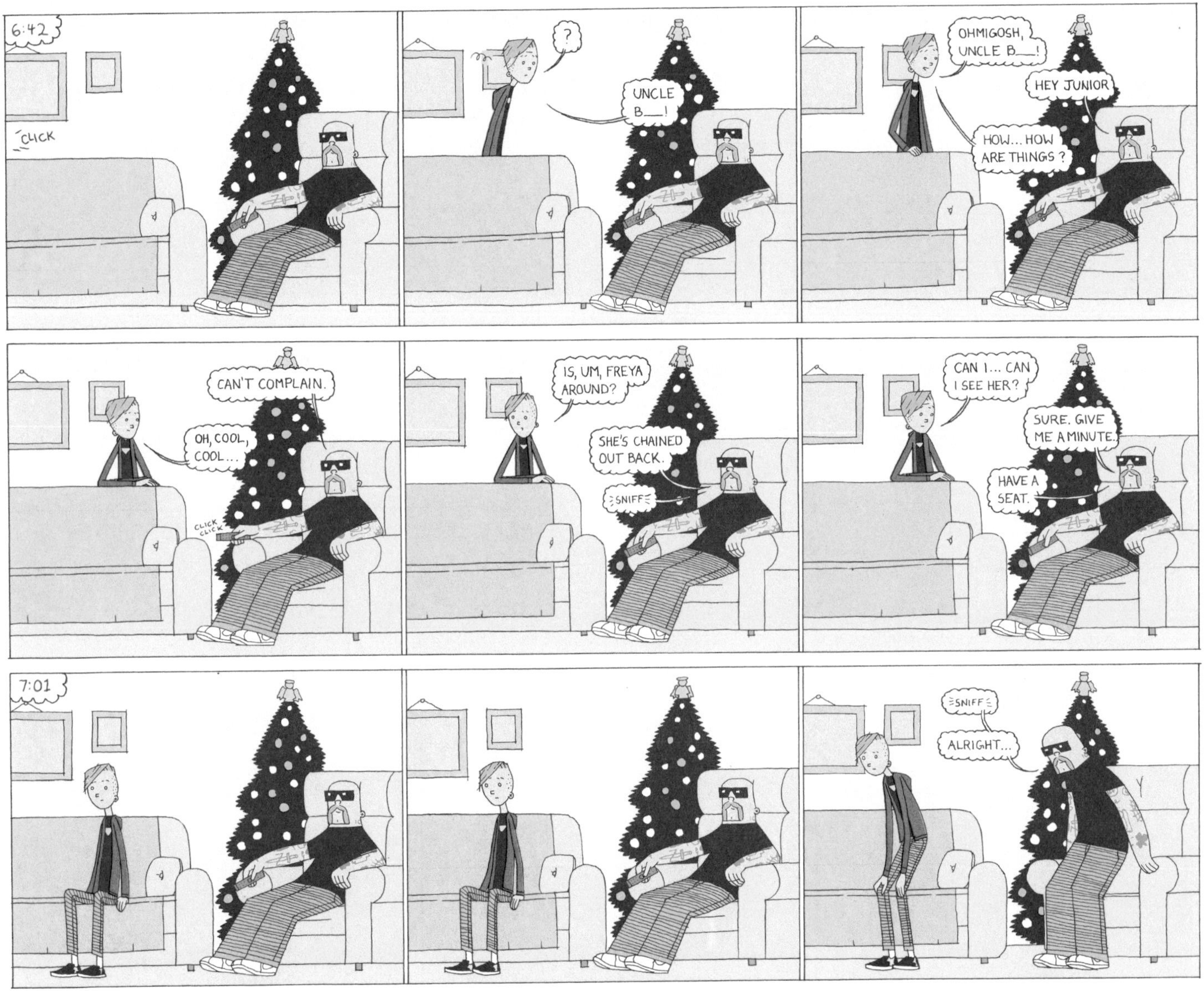
6:42
CLICK
?
UNCLE B__!
OHMIGOSH, UNCLE B__!
HEY JUNIOR
HOW... HOW ARE THINGS?
CAN'T COMPLAIN.
OH, COOL, COOL...
CLICK CLICK
IS, UM, FREYA AROUND?
SHE'S CHAINED OUT BACK.
SNIFF
CAN I... CAN I SEE HER?
SURE. GIVE ME A MINUTE.
HAVE A SEAT.
7:01
SNIFF
ALRIGHT...

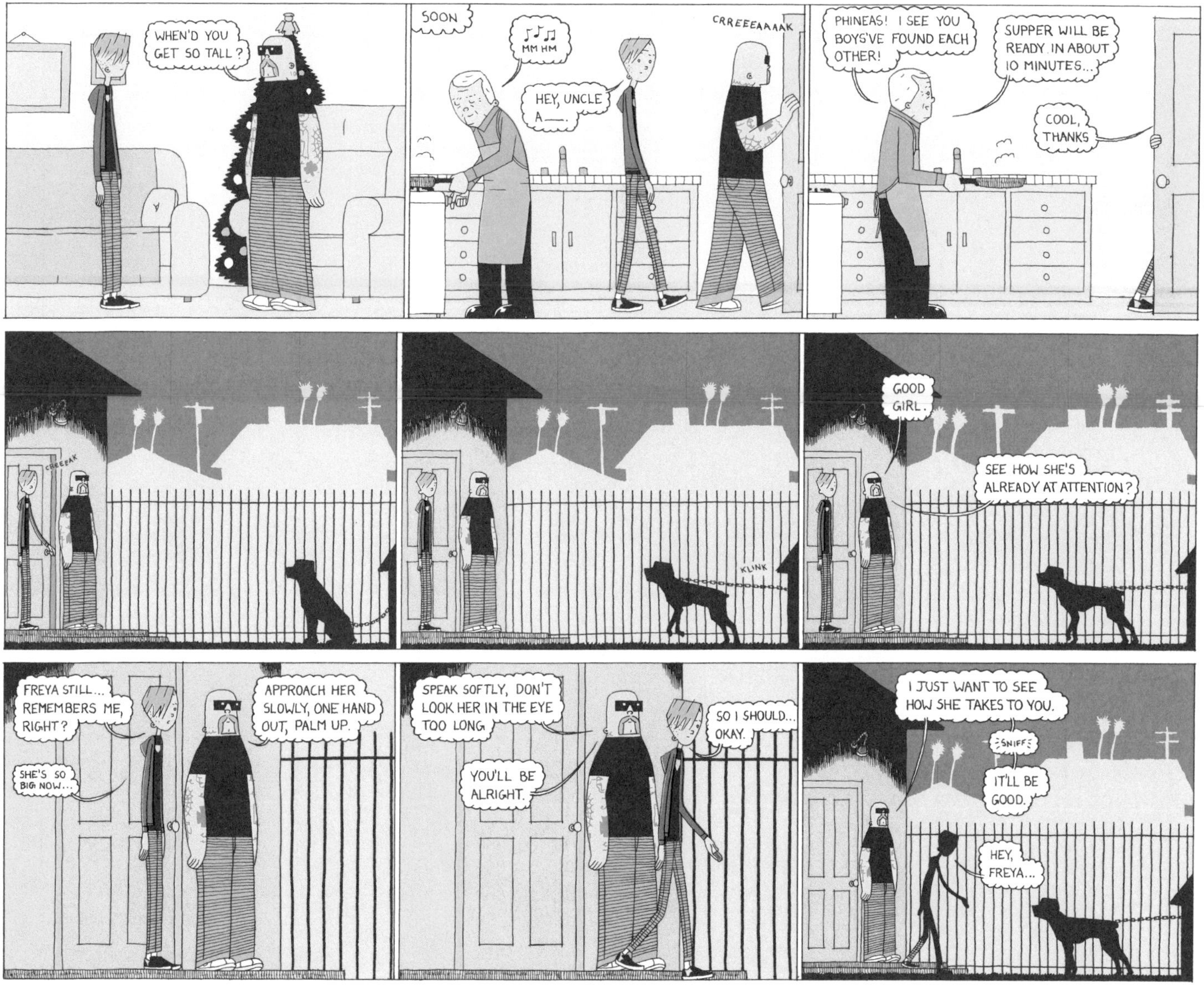
WHEN'D YOU GET SO TALL?
SOON
MM HM
HEY, UNCLE A___.
CRREEEAAAAK
PHINEAS! I SEE YOU BOYS'VE FOUND EACH OTHER!
SUPPER WILL BE READY IN ABOUT 10 MINUTES...
COOL, THANKS
CREEEAK
KLINK
GOOD GIRL.
SEE HOW SHE'S ALREADY AT ATTENTION?
FREYA STILL... REMEMBERS ME, RIGHT?
SHE'S SO BIG NOW...
APPROACH HER SLOWLY, ONE HAND OUT, PALM UP.
SPEAK SOFTLY, DON'T LOOK HER IN THE EYE TOO LONG
YOU'LL BE ALRIGHT.
SO I SHOULD... OKAY.
I JUST WANT TO SEE HOW SHE TAKES TO YOU.
SNIFF
IT'LL BE GOOD.
HEY, FREYA...

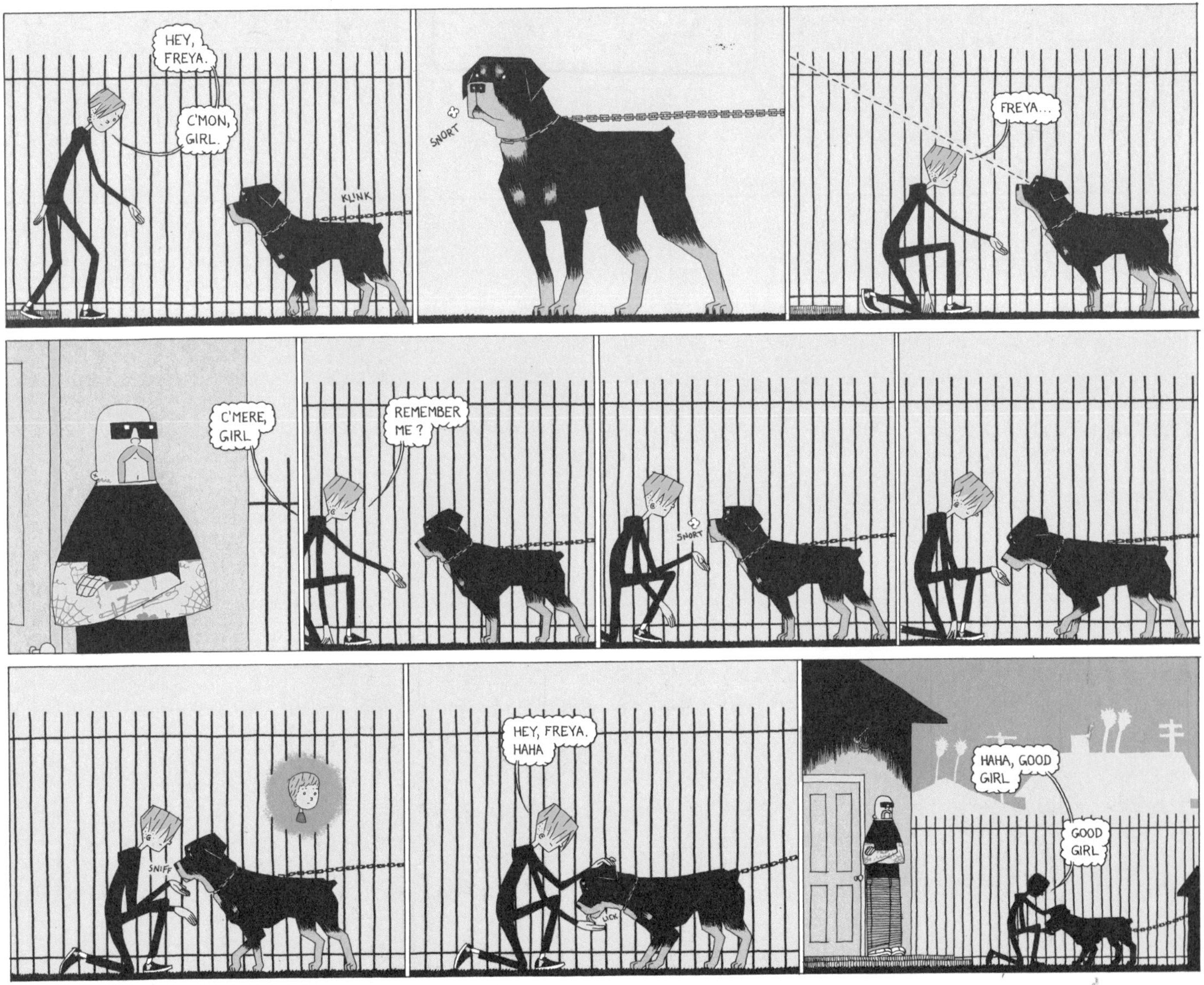
HEY, FREYA.
C'MON, GIRL.
KLINK
SNORT
FREYA...
C'MERE, GIRL
REMEMBER ME?
SNORT
SNIFF
HEY, FREYA. HAHA
LICK
HAHA, GOOD GIRL
GOOD GIRL.